THE ELEMENTS OF THE GODDESS

Caitlín Matthews is a writer working within the Western Mystery Tradition. She has opened new approaches to the Celto-Arthurian tradition with her two volume study of 'The Mabinogion'. Her other books on the Goddess include an anthology on the priesthood of women, *Voices of the Goddess*. She is currently completing a major study of Divine Wisdom, *Sophia, Goddess of Wisdom*.

The *Elements Of* is a series designed to present high quality introductions to a broad range of essential subjects.

The books are commissioned specifically from experts in their fields. They provide readable and often unique views of the various topics covered, and are therefore of interest both to those who have some knowledge of the subject, as well as those who are approaching it for the first time.

Many of these concise yet comprehensive books have practical suggestions and exercises which allow personal experience as well as theoretical understanding, and offer a valuable source of information on many important themes.

In the same series

THE ELEMENTS OF
THE GODDESS

Caitlín Matthews

ELEMENT

Shaftesbury, Dorset ◆ Rockport, Massachusetts

© Caitlín Matthews 1989

First published in Great Britain in 1989 by
Element Books Limited
Longmead, Shaftesbury, Dorset

Second impression 1991

Published in the USA in 1991 by
Element, Inc.
42 Broadway, Rockport, MA 01966

Designed by Jenny Liddle
Cover design by Max Fairbrother
Typeset by Selectmove Ltd, London
Printed in Great Britain by
Billings Ltd, Hylton Road, Worcester

British Library Cataloguing in Publication Data
Matthews, Caitlín 1952–
The elements of the goddess
1. Isis. Worship
I. Title
291.2'11

ISBN 1–85230–085–X

CONTENTS

To the Right Reverends
Olivia Robertson and Lawrence Durdin-Robertson,
Priestess Hierophant and Priest Hierophant of Isis
Founders of the Fellowship of Isis

and

To all who seek the Goddess.

We are entering the time of the nine-pointed star,
the star of making real upon earth
the golden dream of peace that lives within us.

Brooke Medicine Eagle

ACKNOWLEDGEMENTS

My primary debt of gratitude must go to those nameless tradition-bearers, both male and female, incarnate or excarnate, who have preserved and rediscovered the wisdom of the Goddess. Without their patient endurance, this book would never have been written.

The fact that this book appears at all is due to the time which has been made available to me. This statement may seem strange, but all mothers will understand when I thank all those women who have helped me look after my son, Emrys, especially Sandra Mandrey, Ann Cox and Léonie Caldecott. Without their assistance, I could not have managed more than three paragraphs a day. Such foster-mothers are beyond rubies.

To Meinrad Craighead, my God mother-in-law, for companionship on the road.

To the Very Reverends Olivia Robertson and Lawrence Durdin-Robertson, founders of the Fellowship of Isis, for their healing insights which have given me inspiration and confidence to proceed.

To the Reverend Vivienne Vernon-Jones, Priestess-Hierophant of the Lyceum of Isis and Sophia of the Stars, thanks for helping me get back in touch with the Mother.

To Felicity Aldridge, a true exemplar of the Weaver, for her sympathetic support and encouragement.

To my many students whose piercing insights have illumined my way.

To Diarmuid, priest and examplar of the Energiser, for help in Part 1 and for keeping the book on course. His poetic inspiration has made a better woman of me.

To Philip Clayton-Gore, my spiritual brother, who has shown me the face of the Deliverer in a clearer light than I would have ever thought possible.

To all my challengers who have made me focus more clearly on the Goddess and less on myself: their hard wisdom has been a profound source of humility when I have been tempted to get above myself.

To all my readers who have patiently waited for this book. Though this may be one of the shortest, it has also been one of the most difficult books to write, for to please everyone is impossible, and to present the obvious facts about a universally acclaimed deity in her many aspects is a task exceeding a mere 50,000 words.

To Jerry Ozaniec, a truly unsung hero, who helped make me computer literate and who gave up his time to bail me out when I accidentally erased whole chapters.

Lastly, to my dear husband, John, priest of Arianrhod, preserver and protector of my life, for his long understanding and sustaining support. Without him this book would never have been written.

INTRODUCTION

One vision I see clear as life before me, that the ancient Mother has awakened once more, sitting on her throne rejuvenated, more glorious than ever. Proclaim her to all the world with a voice of peace and benediction.

Vivekananda

Within my lifetime, the Goddess has come from obscurity to the forefront of spiritual consciousness. All over the world, people are coming to appreciate and venerate the Divine Feminine principle.

There are now many resources to help the inexperienced find a way to her. There are always new people in each generation, mostly adults – since there are few children who have had what might be called 'a Goddess upbringing' – who want to know the Goddess for themselves. Where do they start?

All of the books currently on the market come from a particular standpoint; from feminism – both radical and Christian – from psychology or from anthropology. Indeed, all books about the Goddess have their own partisan bias. They have been shaped by feminist or psychoanalytical tools and beg questions which may not be those asked by people intent on learning about the Goddess for themselves.

My own standpoint, to be quite clear at the outset, has been that of someone whose cosmology has always included a feminine as well as a masculine divine principle. Over the last twenty-four years, my vision has been shaped by a background of Celtic studies, and a training in the Western esoteric and mystical traditions. My commitment to the Goddess has led me to seek out her wisdom in many aspects of my life.

I freely acknowledge, as all women must, a debt to the courageous and historic liberation which feminism as a political movement has gained for my gender. But I also acknowledge a debt to the traditional guardians of the Goddess's wisdom, whether they be male or female, for these dedicated human beings have kept open the paths to her, often at the cost of their own lives, enabling and encouraging many to follow their example. To those named and nameless mystics, discoverers, writers and practitioners, we all owe a great deal.

The Goddess is usually defined in two ways: by her functions – which are usually classified in terms of the female life cycle – or according to the culture within which she appears. I have chosen to adopt a slightly different approach so that the Goddess alone is my point of reference. I have defined her under a few of her many titles. My intention in so doing is that the reader may approach her directly and form an immediate relationship with her aspects which is not dependent on dualistic ideologies. For the Goddess is the sum of her parts, being both many and indivisible.

I have also made little distinction between the Goddess and her exemplars, her priestesses and heroines, who have been homes for the Goddess and mediators of her many functions. Such women have transcended, or perhaps I should say, transformed their human condition and become real mediators of the Goddess. Similarly, I have included saints and the Blessed Virgin Mary herself in this book, for they also show us aspects of the Divine Feminine and they have the virtue that nearly everyone in the West is familiar with the qualities mediated by them. In choosing this holistic approach, I hope to present a new way of co-operative working with the Goddess which will benefit all newcomers to the temple of her heart.

Every human being is a child of the Goddess. A few years ago I remember picking up a book on the Goddess which said in its opening pages words to the effect, 'Men, if you are reading this book, then put it down now. This is a book for women'. I remember being deeply shocked, since the book purported to be a serious study of the Goddess in her many aspects.

It is true that there are many imbalances in our society, but I believe that the Goddess has re-emerged to help us find ways of restoring creation and of healing divisions, not of making them. Accordingly, in this book, I shall not speak about patriarchy and matriarchy, or seek to lay any blame upon either gender of our species.

The way of the Goddess is one of natural law and natural wisdom. It stems from primordial times and is still being walked by the native peoples of the world. It is a living tradition.

It is primarily the people of the West who are orphans of the Goddess. The social and political reasons for this state of desolation have been documented in many books which deal with the Divine Feminine. Both women and men need to find their Mother, relating to her and her creation in fresh and balanced ways, for every one of us needs to drink of her wisdom and realign ourself with her natural laws.

I have assumed throughout this book that the reader is a member of the human family who seeks the transformative insights which only the Goddess can bring, but who is mature enough to realise that these insights must be shared with other sisters and brothers if the way of the Goddess is to become commonplace in the West.

As the Goddess has not been an integral part of Western life for the last two thousand years, every one of her children is to some extent a disruptive and maladjusted child. Many wonderful and ethically-motivated groups have sprung up which offer ways to find the Goddess. But some have been less balanced and have attempted to dictate fundamental methods of working with or worshipping her. Because the way of the Goddess is unlike other spiritual paths in the West – having no formal or state-administered temples and no organised priesthood – every single person must first find their own way to her. But no one person can claim to own the Goddess or part of her tradition.

This book attempts to help the reader find the Goddess in his or her own way, while also taking into account the difficulties which a twentieth century person has in entering into a relationship with the primal qualities of the Goddess.

A word on the arrangement of the material in this book would, I feel, be useful. Part 1 is really a clearing ground where we look at some of the arguments, opinions and problems that must be dealt with. Here we attempt to clarify our own thoughts, feelings and prejudices about the Goddess. Unless we deal with these first, we will not really be in any fit condition to enter the Temple of the Goddess. In Part 2 we explore the real elements of the Goddess in the light of many of her exemplars. This is the factual and intellectual part of the book, where information is given. Part 3 attempts to go beyond the preceding parts of the book and establish practical methods of working with, and relating to, the Goddess. There is no Part 4, unless you continue the book yourself.

Generally speaking, I have referred directly by name only to each aspect of the Goddess, rather than repeating phrases such as, 'the Tibetan dakini Mamaki', as there is a glossary on Page 121 which lists each Goddess by name and gives details of her country, or culture of origin and specific attribute.

What is written in these pages is necessarily very condensed, due to the format of this series, but with consistent and devoted meditation on the Goddess, you will be able to prove – or disprove – this material for yourself.

If you find what you do not like or cannot accept in these pages, then I hope you will question your response more deeply, for maybe that is precisely the way in which your appropriate response to the Goddess lies. There are such things as 'anti-books', as I call them, texts which outrage you, provoke response and make you want to write your own. Well, go ahead, do it!

If you cannot work with the practical exercises presented on Page 106 in the ways suggested, then find your own ways or adapt them to your own needs. That is what they are for. There is no virtue in the written word unless it can be translated into real experience.

The spirit of the Goddess is all inclusive, compassionate and full of truth. In that spirit, I welcome all readers of whatever sex, race, age or colour to these pages.

A portion of the royalties received from this book will be given each year to charity as my thanksgiving to the Mother for helping to bring this book to birth after a gestation of ten years. It has been a long labour; I now ask the reader to foster this child and make sure it grows up blessedly.

May She be with you wherever you go and guide you your whole life long!

Caitlín Matthews
1st February – 27th March 1989

PART 1
CLEARING THE GROUND

1. THE POWER UNDER THE HILL

There was an old woman lived under the hill
And if she's not gone, she lives there still.
                                    Traditional Rhyme

The advent of a new phase of spirituality is upon us in the shape of the Goddess. Many people are discovering her for the first time, yet for humanity in general this is not something new but the resurgence of a once familiar deity.

The questions arise: where has the Goddess been? why has her archetype been missing for so long from our culture? These are deep questions for which there are no easy answers. The course of spiritual history is not plotted in the same way as we document political or social history; the same rules and criteria cannot be applied.

The fact remains that Western humanity has been without means or access to the Divine Feminine for over a thousand years, except in many little unappreciated ways which we shall be reviewing in the following chapters.

3

This does not mean that the Goddess, in all her aspects, has been absent from us. Rather, it is *we* who have absented ourselves from her. She abides yet, in all her changes and transformations, like the old woman of the nursery rhyme above. She is the power under the hill to whom many have gone in praise, worship and thankfulness as well as in pain, anguish and despair. And yet, many others have never really found the door into that hill. Why not?

If we consider the religious framework of the West, this refusal to consider the possibility of the Divine Feminine is all too clear. It is partially the fault of Christianity, and its marriage to the State, which has uprooted all manifestation of the Goddess and blocked the existing routes to her door.

The Judaic ethos, upon which Christianity was based, as well as Hellenistic philosophy, in whose terms much of Christianity was couched, excluded all aspects of the feminine from the divine to the human, and regarded it as an imperfect channel. When the pagan religions were effectively curtailed in AD 408, access to the Goddess became restricted. It was at about the same time that the inclusion of the Blessed Virgin Mary into the theology of the Church was brought about, although she was revered and respected as the God-bearing Mother rather than worshipped in her own right.

It is easy to apportion blame at Christianity's door, less easy to effect a remedy for the imbalance which has resulted from the wilful exclusion of the Divine Feminine from our culture. Nowadays it is possible to speak of the Goddess as a deity in her own right, but there are still many people who find such talk totally unacceptable. Their objections are that the Goddess is pagan, heathen and full of abomination, and they will frequently quote the scriptures in support of their disapproval. The likelihood that her influence might be regenerative, life-enhancing or beneficial does not occur to them.

To understand the enormous problem which besets the mental attitude of Western civilisation, we need to look at the situation as if the direct opposite were true. Suppose for a moment that the course of spiritual history was reversed. Let us imagine a fictional history in which Christianity was but one of many local cults of the Divine Masculine principle. It might, perhaps, have been localised into a series of cults in which different aspects of deity were promoted, so that there might have been a devotion to the Good Shepherd in one place, and a cult of Christ the Hanged God in another. Many different kinds of people would have perceived the Saviour in different ways, but all would have been serious in their worship. They would have gone to their god in their need, they would have asked him to bless their children, their fields and to receive them kindly after death.

Now let us suppose that a complementary series of cults began to spread and that Emperor Julian (AD 331 to 363) – or Julian the Apostate, as the Christians called him – was Emperor at that crucial time when Constantine the Great headed the great reorganisation of spiritual belief. The Emperor Julian (who would probably have also been called the Great in this fictional account) might have promoted one of these new cults to an aspect of the Goddess. In his case, this would undoubtedly have been one aspect of the Magna Mater, the Great Mother, for example, the Goddess Cybele. Suppose he had declared her worship the official state religion to which everyone must conform. What would have happened?

Undoubtedly there would have been resistance among those who worshipped the Divine Masculine under the form of Christ. But let us suppose that, under Julian's rule, a general abhorrence for male deities pertained and that due to certain well-placed philosophers and theologians, all cults of male deities or female deities not aligned with the worship of Cybele, were to be expunged. Such persistent and devoted worship as there had been would undoubtedly have continued secretly and perhaps been incorporated, in a disguised form, in the new dispensation. Suppose too, that only female priests were tolerated. This would have led to a hierarchy of female prelates, philosophers and theologians.

The polarisation of deity into a prominent Divine Feminine and a recessive Divine Masculine, would have undoubtedly left its own sad marks on our culture. A cult of Cybele's sacrificed lover, Attis (who would not, of course, be accorded divine honours but merely reverence), would perhaps have resulted in enclosures of male, castrated devotees and be played down as being of peripheral importance by the official Goddess party line.

However, let us suppose that despite opposition and resistance, the whole of the Western world expressed at least outward support of the Divine Feminine, and that the idea of a male Divine being was both strange and abhorrent. Perhaps later in time, there would have been a subtle infiltration of the Attis cult by adherents of the cult of Christ, who would attempt to turn 'history' around and claim that God was male.

This extreme and distorted case has exactly mirrored the development of Christianity as a religious influence. I am not stating that such a progression would necessarily be entailed in a Goddess worshipping culture. In fact, things would doubtless be a lot less extreme

5

and much better balanced than this. I have merely given the above example to shock you into rethinking our current predicament.

For the majority of people living in the Western world in the twentieth century, such a being as a Goddess can barely be contemplated as having any validity or spiritual authority. Whether we were brought up as Jews, Christians or subscribe to no belief at all, all of us are influenced by a common mental attitude which it is very hard to shake off.

Even if we are able to rethink our position and accept the fact that all aspects of the Divine Feminine do exist in the same way that the deities of other accepted religions exist, we still have a great problem. To whom do we go for experience of the Goddess? There are no recognised temples, professional priesthoods or sustained traditional practices stemming from the time when the Goddess was a spiritual influence upon the West.

Fortunately, the Goddess herself comes to answer this. Despite the immensity of these problems, the Old Woman under the hill has returned via many channels to help the greatest number of people find their place in the natural laws of the Goddess.

She has come via feminism to remind the world that women have value and potential, and that feminine symbols and images have power. The Goddess has returned at the head of this movement as a meaningful symbol of womens' power.

The Goddess has been used, amongst many other issues, to spearhead political reform, lesbianism, equal rights and better social conditions. What is more, such reforms and reappraisals have met with considerable success; the more so perhaps because of the shock factor of the women's movement. No one expects women to get up and fight, but when they do it is astounding and effective.

Feminine passivity and masculine *laissez-faire* are becoming social attitudes of the past even as I write, although it will be a few hundred years before world-wide consciousness of women's issues is fully established.

So the Goddess has been embroiled in these various issues since time began but, just because we are currently experiencing this radical change in our society, it does not mean to say that the Goddess is limited to political reform or being a figurehead of the women's movement.

She has come via psychoanalysis to heal the split in the Western psyche between the head and the heart, the rational and the intuitive perception. Analysts have encouraged and explored with their clients the myths, stories and images of the Goddess to help the healing of this breach.

The Goddess has come via the orthodox religions in subtle disguises and now returns, unmasked, to shake up stale forms and create movement from within. Christian feminists and women with vocations to the priesthood have brought about a whole new theology of God the Mother which is going to have interesting repercussions in the Christian world.

She has also come via the world of science, where the image and symbolism of the Greek earth goddess, Gaia, has been applied to the living earth itself. This apt symbolic naming, suggested by William Golding to the chief proponent of this theory, the scientist James Lovelock, has had shattering consequences in the West, for it has brought ecological awareness to all levels of society.[53] Now 'green consciousness' prevails, partly because of the fact that humankind can feel more empathy with the plight of Gaia than they ever could for an inert mass of rocks and gases.

All these developments have happened within the twentieth century, which I believe many people will look back upon as a revolutionary time when the Goddess walked among us. What kind of myth will they tell about our time, I wonder?

Why don't you stop reading right now and write a version of that myth, pretending you are a person living several hundreds or thousands of years from now. Write it from your own current perception of the Goddess, even if you don't yet intellectually know who She is. If you don't know how to start, begin with the Old Woman under the hill quoted at the start of this chapter – she'll help you.

2. ADDRESSING THE GODS: REDRESSING THE HUMANS

Unite the male (solar) and female (lunar) energies,
Developing the method of mixing higher and lower energies,
Female assisting male, and male assisting female.

tantric instruction of Lady Yeshe Tsogyel[21]

Let us envisage pure formless Deity. It has no gender or definitions, it just *is*. The metaphorical and symbolic patterns which we apply to deity are masks for our comfort, for our limited human comprehension. The God and the Goddess, the Divine Masculine and Feminine, are like the left and right hands of Deity (metaphorically speaking, of course). This demonstrates immediately how difficult it is to speak in neutral, non-symbolic, language. But this is only one of many confusions which have arisen in our culture.

How do the natures of the Divine Feminine and the Divine Masculine principles differ? If we accept that they are both symbolic emanations of pure Deity, which is imageless and genderless, let us understand them under the titles: the God and the Goddess. Within this duality, unity is also understood – a fact that is readily seen in spiritual symbologies the world over. The usual image is of sexual congress between the male and female forms of Deity, though this is seldom depicted so clearly in Western iconography. The ecstatic experience of human sexuality is one which readily carries over into the symbology of the gods, for it is perhaps the most common – indeed, often our only – experience of non-duality.

The Eastern religions have best conceptualised this understanding in the symbolism of the Yin and Yang, where the black dot of Yin appears in the white half-circle of Yang and the white dot of Yang appears in the black half-circle of Yin. Hindus and Buddhists depict Shiva in the embrace of Shakti – the male and female emanations in actual sexual congress – in tankas (religious instructional paintings) called *yabyum* as a mandala for sacred contemplation: 'All the gods are one god; and all the goddesses are one goddess, and there is one initiator.'[28]

In our discussion of the Goddess, we cannot ignore the Divine Masculine, the God, for he also has a part to play. The myths of the Goddess rarely speak of her in isolation from other deities. Very simplistically, the prime nature of the God is one of stasis: the prime nature of the Goddess is one of movement. Just as we cannot be always standing still or always in motion, neither does our view of the gods remain static or ever-changing.

A kind of 'enantiadromia' is experienced in our world – that is, a succession of complementary opposites, one of which remains recessive while the other is dominant for one part of the cycle and then the polarities reverse. As the dominant and unchanging principle over the past two thousand years has been that of the God – a period when we have ground to ultimate stasis – now we need a strong emphasis on the Goddess to shake things up and rescue us from the stalemate into which we have unthinkingly entered. It is the nature of the Goddess never to rest, but to find the most appropriate and effective means to create. The Goddess has returned to overthrow a lot of stale notions which have been, and indeed still are, considered to be of use in our society.

9

In attempting to find a *thealogy* for the Goddess (*thea* from the Greek refers to the Goddess), all kinds of problems have arisen, not least of which is the further division of the sexes. The lot of women, like that of the Goddess herself, has been one of diminished or suppressed potency. Television quiz games frequently try to pit men and women against each other in tests of physical skill or intellectual dexterity, but they fail to establish the secret potentialities of men and women. Western society is like a reflection of this attitude. Women have their own strengths and skills, as do men, but the difference between these skills is neither qualitative nor quantitative – it is complementary.

The complementary abilities of any species are easily discerned by the most amateur naturalist. The adaptive nature of humankind is also fairly obvious. We have seen what are considered to be natural functions of one sex become the province of the other sex, for example during the First World War, where women proved to be extremely capable of driving motor vehicles, farming, mining and a variety of other jobs which had hitherto been considered to be suitable for men only. Here the complementary and adaptive qualities of humankind were manifesting themselves quite naturally – if there is a dearth of men, women must fulfil the need. Twentieth century society has shown that women can, and do, perform all kinds of functions which only a hundred years ago were considered too onerous or unsuitable for them.

There is nothing more irritating than to be pigeon-holed as a function. When strangers ask you, 'what do you do?' they usually mean 'where can I file you?' Women have been filed under 'children' and 'home' for a long, long time, and are likely to appear under this heading for an indefinite period as, despite the indisputable fact that as a species we may adapt almost endlessly, it is clear that men are never going to bear children, only father them. However, women are capable of many other activities as well.

During the raising of feminine consciousness in the middle part of the twentieth century, men have come under increasing attack, being perceived as aggressors and heavy-handed patriarchs, the full burden of responsibility for female suppression being placed on their shoulders. Some men have responded sensitively to these accusations and tried to find ways of redress. Being born a man has begun to be seen, in some circles, as an ultimate misfortune!

Just for a moment, stop and consider what your life to date would have been like if you had been born into a different gender, race or species. if you can really empathise sufficiently to identify yourself with a gender, race or species which you consciously or unconsciously dislike, you will immediately see that life cannot proceed along these lines of imbalance, nor can one section of society be expected to bear the responsibility for karmic debts. Our dualistic upbringing prompts us to polarise everything into the categories: ourselves and our opinions are considered to be good, and those that we dislike or disagree with are bad. Whether you see feminism as the hand of the Goddess setting things in balance or else as a load of hysterical women getting excited about nothing, it has undeniably made its impact. It is for us to be sensitive and aware of each other as human beings first of all, and to allow love and consideration to enter into every relationship. For that is the love which the Goddess brings: she despises no part of her creation.

Men do not need to go cap in hand either to women or to the Goddess, they just need to accord each due respect. For men can have their own relationship with the Goddess, just as women do. It seems, to date, that women have had all the fun getting to know the Goddess and finding out about how they relate to her. They have workshops and women's mystery days, menstrual seminars and fire-festival picnics – all of which are intense, uproarious, and Dionysian. If women return from such events intoxicated with their own power, it should be regarded, on one level, as the equivalent of a man returning from the pub where he's had a great time with his mates. These kind of celebrations of womanhood have not been available for many hundreds of years in the West: so men should consider how they would feel after that time!

Given the feminist climate, a lot of men have been dissuaded from too much in-depth exploration of the Goddess on their own because she has seemed to belong primarily to women. But this need not be the case. The heart of the Goddess is a temple to which we need only walk along the path leading from our own heart. If desire speeds you towards the Goddess, follow your thought.

Some people seem to imagine that woman equals Goddess. This confusion has arisen over a long period, although it is really a question of metaphor.

The manner in which we understand the gods is complex, using a symbolic language of the imagination which unfortunately is very often misinterpreted and applied literally. For example, the Goddess is not the earth, although the earth may be a very good image with which to represent her.

However we like to see her, the Goddess is not a person, although we may visualise her in one of her many anthropomorphic images. The earliest primal peoples of prehistory made few representations of the gods, but the Goddess is clearly visible as the Mother, her fecund form bursting with life. Other peoples saw her as the land itself, venerating certain land-features such as hills, stream and lakes as if they were the Goddess.

The Goddess is (like) the earth, we may say. But soon the simile is dropped and becomes a metaphor which we readily accept. In this book, I have attempted to keep the symbolic channels very obvious so that we remain alert to the difficulties of careless thinking.

The Goddess is primarily a spiritual channel reaching down into our soul. We apply the pronoun 'she' to what is appreciably a Divine Feminine stream of wisdom. Because the pronoun and images are female, this does not automatically empower all women everywhere to become or act like goddesses. People of all kinds have been turning to her for help on all levels since the beginning of time. The Goddess is not a woman, although a woman's form is one of the many garments she may choose to wear.

Our confused and dualistic society has mistaken the way of the Goddess as being only appropriate for women. This shows a confusion of levels and polarities which we must try and get straight at the outset. The old symbolic trap awaits those who venerate the Goddess in the same way that it did for those who venerated the Divine Masculine: God is God, not man; Goddess is Goddess, not woman.[81]

In *The Western Way: The Hermetic Tradition*[66] I explained how it is a mistake to think that only women can mediate the Divine Feminine, and only men can mediate the Divine Masculine. Mediation is a technical term for the reception and transmission of an energy, in this case, divine energy. You probably know many people who are natural mediators of different energies: that is, they are tuned to the archetypes which typify their own innate abilities. For example, my late aunt was the very soul of sensitivity and I always used to think of her as the mediator of Iris, the messenger of the Greek Goddess Hera, who often had to undertake difficult missions. I also have a friend who is very obviously the mediator of Minerva, the Goddess of wisdom, although he might seem to be of the 'wrong' gender to many.

The traditional esoteric teaching on this matter is unequivocal: there are deities and there are mediators. We can work with anyone who is appropriate for us. In esoteric groups who actively use god-forms in their rituals, it is indeed normal to cast a man as a male god-form and a woman as a female one, but there are mighty exceptions to this rule when, from natural ability or as a training exercise, a man is cast, for example, as the Goddess Hathor or a woman as the God Enlil.

In the last analysis, it is not the form which matters, but the energy or power being mediated. Energies, by nature, have no gender: love, strength, insight, justice or protection being neither more nor less suitable to men than to women.

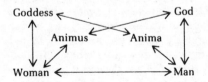

Goddess ⟷ God	DIVINE LEVEL
Animus ⟷ Anima	ARCHETYPAL LEVEL
Woman ⟷ Man	HUMAN LEVEL

The Divine, Archetypal and Human Polarities

As this diagram shows, the manner in which we perceive and mediate the energies of Goddess and God are simple, yet subtle. Each level has its balanced partnership making up a whole. God and Goddess make up the divine level. Woman and Man constitute the Human level. While inbetween are the transpersonal daimons of anima and animus making up the Archetypal level. I have borrowed the words anima and animus from Jungian psychology as convenient terms for this explanation. The Greeks called the beings of this archetypal level *daimons*, meaning indwelling spirits who help and inspire us. A man has an anima, conceived of as an ideal inner woman. A woman has an animus, conceived of as an ideal inner man. These twin images haunt our imagination and often make our love-lives incredibly tortuous until we realise that these *daimons* will never become physical realities.[60] They are messengers between the divine realms and the human levels of our experience.

The dynamics of this diagram show the complex relationships which we can have with the gods and with each other. A man can relate to a woman on a physical level, to the Divine Masculine on a spiritual level, and via his anima he can relate to the Goddess; or he can perceive the Goddess more subtly through a woman. A woman can relate physically to a man, directly and spiritually to the Goddess, and she can perceive the features of the God through her animus; or indeed by relationship with a man.

Of course, the esoteric pathologies of homosexual men and women are more varied and do not always conform to this heterosexual model. Homosexuality has never been despised within the mysteries of the Goddess where Divine Feminine and Masculine powers have been internally balanced. The androgynous or transsexual nature of esoteric mediation has often been recognised as a particularly potent basis for a shamanic vocation.[101]

There is also the question of approach: do men and women ap-proach the Goddess in different ways? Historical testimony witnesses that they surely do. Separate cults of the Goddess for men and women were certainly part of the ancient world at different times. The cult of the Roman Goddess Bona Dea was administered by Vestal Virgins and attended solely by women. So carefully were these mysteries guarded that no one today has any idea of what they really involved. In con-trast, the cult of the Thracian Goddess Cybele, though it had female as well as male priests, was mainly typified by its ecstatic priesthood, the *galloi*, who castrated themselves in honour of the Goddess. This cult is a prime example of how the view that 'all souls are feminine to the Supreme Reality' has a tendency to become manifest.

Whatever public ritual or cult activity we choose to engage in today, there are still distinctly different approaches to the Divine Feminine. As we saw in the previous diagram, women have a direct and familiar association with the Goddess; for men, the Goddess is more awesome and less immediately approachable. Women have the support of mythic symbolism which associates their life cycle with that of the phases of the moon, and the corresponding phases or aspects of the Goddess. These aspects, usually defined as Maiden, Mother and Crone, have been outlined in many books, courses and workshops and for many women they represent the valid basis of a whole theology which is practically and personally applicable.[99]

This understanding was current even in Pythagoras' day: 'Women give to each successive stage of their life the same name as a god; they call the unmarried woman Maiden (*Kore*), the woman given in marriage to a man Bride (*Nymphe*), her who has borne children Mother (*Meter*) and her who has borne children's children Grand-mother (*Maia*).'[38] If we reverse this statement we find, of course, that many of the Goddess' titles derive from the life cycle of women. Yet women may be of any age and still mediate the different qualities or aspects of the Goddess during each stage within their life cycle.

Men, however, clearly cannot operate experientially in the same way, and therefore a different approach is necessary. As outlined in the diagram, men have a direct line to the Divine Masculine but they also stand in dynamic relationship to the Goddess. The Divine Feminine is focused through the burning glass of the anima. If a man can disentangle this archetypal level from the human level, and not project the anima upon a physical woman, he can associate with the Goddess via this route.

In the ancient mysteries, this understanding was fully utilised and the male initiate was paired with a priestess who taught him through all the levels. An account of such a training is partially expounded in Dion Fortune's novels *The Sea Priestess*[30] and *Moon Magic*.[29] Today such a training scheme is virtually impossible for not only are there insufficient fully trained priestesses, but moral values have taken a mighty shift since ancient times. The esoteric teaching on this problem of approach is clearly imparted in the essay, 'The Worship of Isis', in Dion Fortttune's *Aspects of Occultism*:

> Each woman is a priestess of the Goddess. She is the potent queen of the underworld, whose kisses magnetize and give life. In the inner she is all-potent, she is the fertiliser. She causeth the male to create, for without desire, life goes not forth.
>
> Man should not be for ever potent, but lie latent in the arms of Persephone, surrending himself. Then she who was dark and cold as outer space before the creative Word, is made queen of the underworld, crowned by his surrender, and her kisses become potent upon his lips.[28]

The understanding which lies at the heart of this teaching is a hard one for some men to accept: that the Goddess and her priestessly representatives are in a position of power, that the time has come to listen to the Goddess' wisdom and to learn from her.

Men experience the Goddess through their creative side. She makes manifest their ideas by animating their dormant creativity. There is a strong sense of ebb and flow about these energies which give men an experience of the cyclical nature of the feminine menstrual cycle. This kind of relationship is rarely recognised for what it is, yet all men can discover and welcome this experience. Although the effect of the Goddess upon a man is less immediately physical than in a woman, it is nonetheless potent.

In Part 2, I have presented a method of approach which is equally workable by both men and women, and which does not conflict with any existing methods of approach, but which can be synthesised with them.

3. FINDING A MYTH TO LIVE BY

There can be no world without direction. The gods have names and places
in the compass. By calling their names, they go to their places – their homes.

Wija, a Balinese shadow-puppeteer

The way in which we come to the gods has largely been forgotten.
This is why psychotherapists are so busy trying to process and in-
terpret our fleeting dreams for us, to find the archetypal forces of the
gods in our often confused and ill-motivated lives.

Jungian analysis shows how the working out of our complexes often follows an archetypal or mythical parallel. Those analysts who
have followed the lead of C. G. Jung have found his theory of the
collective unconscious significant and useful. This theory states that
all of us have access to a wider framework of symbolic, mythic or
archetypal references that can be supplied by either genetic heritage or cultural programming. This means, according to Jung, that
our dreams and mythic scenarios often accord with this collective
symbolic unconscious level.

Thus, the woman who finds herself in a restricted relationship into
which no light seems to penetrate may be said to be archetypally

identified with Persephone, Queen of the Underworld. Likewise, the man who enjoys a wild round of female company without any sense of responsibility may be working out a Zeus-like existence. When appropriate mythical stories are told to people with these same archetypal imbalances, the problem is identified and brought to the surface where it can be worked through.[51] At least, that is the theory.

Here, no one is implying that men and women are gods, only that they sometimes experience life through the focus of a particular deity or aspect of deity. This is, of course, a different way of looking at spirituality, where we might normally focus our attention consciously on one deity or one aspect of deity and, according to our guiding mystical principle, attempt to *identify spiritually* with or enter into some kind of relationship with deity.

However, the question remains: where are we going to find the Goddess? How can we, as adult women or men, go about discovering how she fits into our lives?

The Goddess is like a never-ending story that we may invite into the circle of our lives by the mere mention of her name. How we respond to the subsequent story she makes within us is another matter. But where do we find such a story?

There are few surviving Goddess-worshipping traditions in the West. The remnants of our neolithic heritage went underground over two millennia ago. The pagan revival has had to use the information supplied by archaeology, anthropology and linguistic scholarship to represent the mysteries of the Goddess to the twentieth century.[47] Goddess communities and groups in the West today derive their impetus from stories appearing in ancient mythologies, folk stories and neglected scriptures of archaic religions.

We are conditioned to think of myth, story and scripture as three different things. For many people, a 'myth' is an untruth; for others, it represents redundant scripture; stories are considered to be appropriate for children, the bedridden or the blind; while scripture is the prop and stay of the devout. Myth, story and scripture, however, are all forms of texts to live by.

Many people, struggling with childhood models of spirituality, may find it impossible to approach the Goddess in anything other than a cautious or fearful way. They may have read accounts of the Goddess which have been transmitted via the theologians and apologists of other 'rival' spiritual traditions, in which the whole feminine archetype from the Goddess down to women themselves is presented in a less than favourable light. The political manipulation of spiritual traditions has frequently warped the story, myth or saving text of the Goddess out of true. How does this affect our own search for a story?

Let us consider the possibilities. There are the surviving mythologies of the ancient world, remnants of traditions which are no longer animated by surviving veneration (if we discount modern revivals.) There are the living Goddess traditions of the world in places such as Africa, India and Japan, where they remain part of tribal society or exist under the umbrella of one of the major world faiths. There are the Goddess stories and traditions which have been reanimated and reworked by both modern pagan religions and feminists. These usually draw upon rich traditions which are then subtly rewoven to yield a sub-text which is supportive of that group's needs. Merlin Stone's, *Ancient Mirrors of Womanhood* is a good example of mythology rewritten for feminist use.[92,19]

In finding a myth of the Goddess to live by, it is important to find the right criteria. If we choose to work with ancient mythologies of the Goddess, we must not live in our own ancestral past, whether or not we perceive this to be a golden matriarchy, or an egalitarian society in which men and women lived amicably together.[90,25] We live in the twentieth century, and there has been rather a lot of water under the bridge since those days. Some people may not find it appropriate, for example, to invoke the Goddess to make them fertile. In ancient times, children supported the tribal framework and such prayers were commonplace (and still useful for infertile couples). However, in a time when over-population and effective methods of birth-control have changed our social structure, where women are released from continuous child-bearing, other levels of fertility must also be sought after.

If we choose to work within the framework of existent Goddess religions, as Rita Gross suggests in her essay 'Hindu Female Deities as a Resource',[36] we must realise that there may be symbolic and cultural problems which we had not considered. It takes a very long time to be symbolically at home within a religion whose cultural basis is different from one's own.

If we draw upon the reanimated Goddess myths of the twentieth century revival, we may find ourselves at odds with the controversial way in which the sub-text may have been written or else we may be distrustful of the authenticity of such reworked stories.

There is truly only one criteria in such a choice: *does it work for you?* We may find our mythic format, our story, our saving text, from a combination of all these approaches. It may take a very long time to well up into our consciousness. In the course of this book, I hope you will begin to find the traces of a spiritual path or else find new approaches to an old mythical scenario.

We should be aware that finding our personal Goddess myth is a matter of asking continual questions. Perhaps one of the first questions to spring up will be: 'on what authority do we base our myth and is it trustworthy?' Trust and confidence only come when our chosen myth has been tested and found to be supportive, but to start with, we must act according to a basic premise: we must behave 'as if' the myth was trustworthy. These important words give us the faith to begin. The question of authority is very much tied to our own self-image and confidence; if we don't believe in ourselves, we won't be able to believe in our personal myth. It is indeed a circular business!

The rule of the Goddess is that there are no rules. Finding your personal myth is a matter of what works for you and how you respond with skilful wisdom when your motherwit is stimulated. Some people have a very conservative approach indeed and need heavily stated guidelines to proceed. Such an approach is not very successful, for the Goddess should percolate through our lives in very spontaneous ways. She gives us the space to say to ourselves: 'it's all right to do this'. Granting or allowing ourselves space to operate is a matter of personal freedom and leaping free from self-imposed restraints and boundaries.

The next question to ask once you have started should be: 'is the myth challenging enough?' We instinctively respond to myths which mirror our own condition in some way, and it is very easy to choose a myth which makes you feel too comfortable. The myth can very easily become a straitjacket or a prison unless we continually reassess our changing situation. Escaping from a myth that we have outgrown and whose energy has no longer the power to animate us, into a myth which is dynamic and challenging to our evolving self is very important. A sensitive approach to this transformation of the myth can be found in *Personal Mythology* by David Feinstein and Stanley Krippner.[27]

4. HER SECOND COMING

The goddess will not necessarily involve herself in her
second coming with the same activities she has undertaken in past
or current goddess religions. She may, but she may also manifest
solutions for totally new problems.

'Hindu Female Deities as a Resource for the Contemporary
Rediscovery of the Goddess'
Rita M. Gross

There are many real problems for seekers of the Goddess' wisdom
which are seldom addressed because the Goddess is such a new
concept to many people, and because there are currently few opportunities to learn from or train with people who do have experience of
the Goddess. In this section, we will look searchingly at Goddess
spirituality and attempt to define some of those problems.

There are many ways in which the Goddess is returning to our
world, but every one of these depends very urgently on how we
visualise her and what kind of response we activate as a result of this.
The re-formation of the Goddess amongst us will depend upon what
we think and feel about her, for we stand at an important crossroads
in human comprehension of the divine.

If we look at the history of spiritual concepts we see that two kinds of
spiritual expression result: an esoteric and an exoteric response. Exoteric spirituality represents the basic common denominator of accepted
belief; it operates with a limited, often narrow, set of guide-lines and
images. The greater part of spiritually-operative people practise the

exoteric side of their belief: they go to church or synagogue but they are not generally involved in the more mystical side of spiritual practice. They rarely stray beyond vocal and petitionary prayer and regard meditation or deeper spiritual commitment as the task of professionals. Exoteric practitioners operate from the standpoint that they are separate from their deity.

Esoteric spirituality, on the other hand, represents the mystical understanding of belief; it operates from the inside outwards, and is at home in all of the many levels of its images and concepts. Within every spiritual tradition, esoteric practitioners constitute a small percentage of believers. These esoteric people may include mystics of deep insights, saints or those whose lives reflect in the everyday world the blessedness of their spiritual source. For esoteric practitioners, there is little or no division between themselves and their deity.

We are currently seeing an unfortunate rise in spiritual fundamentalism throughout the world which suppresses the esoteric and mystical understanding of belief, and frequently warps mysticism for political ends. Esoteric practice is likewise considered of little worth, and the spiritual forms (number of prayers said, number of services attended and so on) are even more rigidly defined.

If you think that the spiritual problems of the world have little to do with the Goddess, then you are wrong. A fuller appreciation of the Divine Feminine in many forms is breaking through every level of life and it is already possible to see the same kind of development we have just described. We have Goddess religion, Goddess mystics, Goddess believers and, may she help us, Goddess fundamentalists too!

This is also clearly manifest in some contemporary approaches to the Goddess, where the image of the almighty patriarchal Jehovah has been the model for a vengeful matriarchal Mother Goddess. While it is unlikely that the full range of the Goddess' powers could ever operate via such intolerant models as this, it is worth bearing in mind that the kind of forms, images and concepts which we create concerning the Goddess will have significant effect upon future generations. It is up to us to avoid bequeathing the worst of the spiritual legacy which we inherited to our own children. This leads us on to another problem which faces us: in what spirit do we set out to bring about the second coming of the Goddess? Is our existing spiritual framework wide enough to encompass the Goddess, or are we expected to start from scratch?

Even though our spiritual conditioning may be of a specific nature, for example Christian or Jewish, this should not be a barrier to our progress just because we are struggling to throw away one set of ideas and take on another. We must understand that it is not possible to make a clean break between spiritual traditions and that the spiritual imprinting of our childhood need not work against us.

I believe that the problems which are encountered during this first spiritual contact with the Goddess are often overlooked. At this critical moment, when we seek to revise our spirituality, our expectations are very high. Unfortunately, our corresponding spiritual resources are also limited. Without clear guidance, it is often impossible to proceed with any confidence. It is like learning to swim in deep water without an instructor. We must remember that it is permissible to wear waterwings! While there are many who have learned to swim by dint of throwing themselves in the deep end, far more have sunk without trace.

If you are a devotee of an orthodox religion at heart or have the preconditioning of a tradition you have abandoned, the Divine Feminine – whether you see her as the Goddess or not – does not require you to jettison your current beliefs or your spiritual training. It is easier for spiritual energy to pass along already existent channels than it is for it to pass through a rock face which you are in the process of mining. But spiritual energy, like water, soon wears its own channels and however you venerate the Goddess, new ways will open up.

The discipline of various spiritual traditions provides scaffolding on which the seeker learns to move about. If you have never moved off that scaffolding into the divine space which it encloses, you may well need to dismantle it in order to set up a fresh structure. If, however, you are already confident within the divine vastness you will not need me to tell you that the Goddess is already there.

While some aspects of other spiritual traditions can be helpful, monotheist models of orthodox religion are not the best basis on which to found an understanding of the Goddess. One of the main problems for the Westerner wishing to venerate the Goddess is that the West does not comprehend a deity who has several aspects, or even allow a polarised pair of Divine Feminine and Divine Masculine deities.

Aspectual deity is a part of Eastern tradition. We see its manifestation in Hinduism, for example, where godhead itself is formed of three functional powers: Creator, Preserver and Destroyer in the persons of Brahma, Vishnu and Shiva and their polarised consorts, Sarasvati, Lakshmi and Parvati. Mystical Christianity itself retains traces of aspectual deity – although theologians would hardly agree with this definition – in the persons of the saints. Even the doctrine of the Trinity – God as Father, Son and Holy Spirit – which stands at the centre of Christian belief, gives us an idea of how the Western tradition has attempted to gloss over the older pagan understandings.

Monotheism is not an understanding that is natural to humankind. Even within mystical Islam, Allah has a hundred names and

' according to Shah Ni'matullah Wali, the four angels Gabriel, Michael, Seraphiel and Azrael correspond to the four aspects of the name Allah. The four letters A L L H correspond to the mystic's Heart, Intellect, Spirit and Soul'.[5]

As we discovered earlier, the Goddess cannot be fully understood under one specific image for she permeates the whole creation. If we approach her from just one standpoint we teeter on the brink of making her in our image, or of limiting her to a particular set of symbols. For though we speak of the Divine Feminine as 'the Goddess', we should really be finding her in many different ways, through spontaneous metaphors which arise in our own experience, and in many aspects both known and unknown.

Our expectations of the Goddess will necessarily derive from the kind of mythic framework or story in which we work. We cannot expect, however, that every image, every aspect of the Goddess will be equally valid for our contemporary condition. Some are going to be more useful than others, but the fact that there is more than one set of images soon becomes obvious.

We may find it hard to approach the Goddess in any meaningful way because we just don't know how to begin, or because we never had any kind of spiritual training. People who proceed from this basis are perhaps the most fortunate, although they may also feel themselves to be the most disadvantaged. They have no previous models to reconcile or reject, but neither have they yet learnt any skilful methods. I hope that the last part of this book and the ensuing exercises will help them to find a practical wisdom which is both adaptable and supportive.

One of the prime questions which we all encounter is: 'where does the Goddess fit into things?' We sometimes lack any real sense of the Goddess because she has no immediate cosmology, mythology, or thealogy. Yet, we live in a time which is going to supply these, either by redefinition of ancient or existing models, or by dint of sheer spiritual contact with the Goddess herself. Until that time, however, we must find our own. While our belief in the existence of the Goddess may seem the most important thing at this stage, there may still be worries about her origins, her nature, her acts and so on. Some parts of our mind may be perturbed that the Goddess is 'a new thing'; we may wonder whether we are subscribing to a concept which has been re-invented and re-invested with meaning.

These are valid concerns which should serve to keep us ever alert to the fact that the Goddess is reappearing in many new ways, often using people or movements whom we personally dislike in order to establish herself in the living world once more. However, the fact that the Goddess has never left us, but that we have ignored her, is more to the point.

There is a Yoruba proverb that says: 'Where there are no people, there is no divinity'.[78] The weight and authority which existing deities and religious traditions carry is built up over hundreds of years of practice and belief. We live in a time when the revisioning of Goddess spirituality is already taking place. Our role is to find the most effective methods of co-operating with her in order to establish a strong and supportive tradition.

Some may enquire, along with D. L. Carmody, 'whether the Goddess does not represent an intellectual regression, for all that she may represent an emotional advance?'[81] The old dualistic notions which see the Goddess as fickle, unstable and the product of a corrupt pagan world are hard to shift. The only answer to this is to find out to what degree our society is willing to change. For radical change is necessary if we are truly afraid of losing our intellectual superiority over creation at the cost of fostering the compassion of the Goddess.

In all these fears and anxieties about spiritual error and orientation, it is important to establish one ground rule: the prime directive of the Goddess, as with all the forms of deity, is that she is neither good nor evil. Deity is a power, an energy, a force. The Goddess may appear in wrathful or challenging forms, but these should not be considered as hostile. She is the kernel of truth at the heart of everything and if she appears in challenging forms to you, look more deeply, considering why this may be so. Many of those who venerate the Goddess are unhappy about her supposedly dark aspects because they dualistically associate 'dark' with 'evil'. In order to save her child about to do something dangerous or silly, a mother will get angry, shout or scream, but this doesn't mean to say that she loves her child any less.

The old, outworn, dualistic concept of the Goddess as cruel and capricious must be viewed for what it is: a reflection of our shadow-side, a terrible polarisation of social responsibility with which women have been burdened as a sex. The reverse image of the Goddess as all sweetness and light is likewise a dubious model on which to build. The Goddess has dynamic strength and transformative wisdom as well as enfolding compassion.

The Goddess stands at the heart of life, death and further existence and she will assume the forms which are most appropriate in her dealings with our world. If you are prepared to discover these forms, you will become an instrument of her second coming, a mediator of her compassion both in your own time cycle and in the aeons waiting to be born of her womb.

Part 2
Visioning the Temple

5. INNER
CONSTELLATION

Those who call upon Isis in faith claim that they do indeed
behold her in her manifold epiphanies
Oxyrhynchus Litany[97]

In this part of the book, we begin to outline the shape of the Goddess, calling upon our mental and visual powers to help us comprehend the incomprehensible. In using any image, glyph or diagram to describe the Goddess, we are using what is little more than a crutch that helps us to get along until we can walk on our own feet by the light of indwelling wisdom. Until that shines from within us, regard what follows as a theoretical cosmology of the Goddess, a working model, and no more.

The Goddess is composed of many aspects: she is as many-faced as a jewel. Her manifestations are so various that there is no universal language or symbology which can adequately clothe her power. We are going to try to find a common language in this section so that, regardless of mythology, cultural conditioning, education or the lack of it, the Goddess will shine her impartial light upon us all.

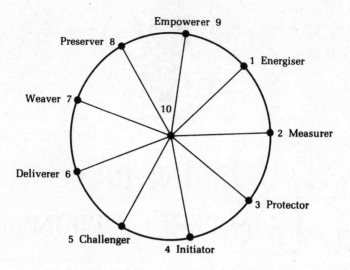

Fig. 1 The Shaper of All (no.10) and Her Ninefold Aspects

Visualise far above you, a distant source of light which shines like a great star in the darkness. As it shimmers above you, the star seems to spin, sending off a catherine wheel of sparks. It is as though the star has sent nine satellites of itself down through the night sky, which hang perfectly constellated below the central star, yet millions of miles above your head.

Feel the intensity of light which the star and its satellite constellation beams down upon you. You are experiencing the full illumination of the Goddess in a visualised image, for the central star is none other than the Goddess as the Shaper of All, the originator of all things, and the ninefold constellation shining below the star are her Ninefold Aspects.

Imagine that you are looking directly above at the shape that this makes (see Fig.1).

The star which is the Shaper of All has nine aspects, each of which has a function. Very basically expressed, they work in this way:

1. **THE ENERGISER** gets things moving.

2. **THE MEASURER** defines the limits.

3. **THE PROTECTOR** guards those limits.

4. **THE INITIATOR** deepens experience, re-creating things.

5. **THE CHALLENGER** opposes and questions in order to get things growing, but also destroys what is stale and outworn.

6. **THE DELIVERER** brings liberation.

7. **THE WEAVER** makes connections.

8. **THE PRESERVER** feeds and nourishes.

9. **THE EMPOWERER** brings wisdom.

To give us some notion of the way in which these aspects appear, I have enumerated below the many aspects of Mary, the Blessed Virgin. While some may consider this either blasphemous or inappropriate to a study of the Goddess, Mary is a valid form in which the Divine Feminine has been appearing continuously since the Goddess was last officially venerated in the West and this makes her a valuable link with our heritage. Even if one is not Christian, these aspects of Mary are sufficiently part of the living Western tradition for most people to understand.

Both Mary and the Egyptian Goddess Isis are linked by sympathetic cords of story and circumstance, some of which we will be discovering as we proceed through the Temple of Light. They are both helpful to us, for they portray the full range of aspects which we will be encountering in the following pages. Because they are both well-known and established forms of the Divine Feminine (regardless of the official Christian view), they show us a coherent pattern.

THE ASPECTS OF MARY, THE BLESSED VIRGIN

SHAPER OF ALL: Within medieval tradition there are many statues of the kind called Vièrge Ouvrante. These represent the Blessed Virgin as a wooden statue, the front of her body opening, like a pair of doors, to reveal the Trinity inside her, so that God the Father, Son and Holy Spirit appear to have originated from her substance.

ENERGISER: At the wedding of Cana, Mary is the one responsible for the manifestation of her son's first public ministry. She points out that the wine has run out and asks him to accomplish the miracle of turning water into wine.

MEASURER: According to the non-canonical *Proto-Evangelium*,[45] Mary and her companions are chosen to weave the new veil for the temple. Lots are cast, and she draws the red and purple – the royal colours – indicative of her destiny.[45]

PROTECTOR: The most common representation of Mary as Protector is under her title of *Mater Misericordia*, which shows her holding out her mantle under which shelter her suppliants. She shows herself as Protector also in the flight into Egypt, when she escapes with her son and St Joseph from Herod's soldiers.

INITIATOR: As the Virgin of the Nativity, Mary shows herself as Initiator, that is she bestows on Jesus her own mortality, teaching him its ways, in order to bring about the Redemption.

CHALLENGER: A little-known folk-hymn, *The Bitter Withy*, which draws upon a Gnostic tradition, tells how Jesus was taunted by rich men's children for his humble birth in a stable. In retaliation he demonstrated his superior abilities by making a bridge out of sunlight over which the children ran and drowned. The consequence of this was:

> So Mary mild fetched home her child,
> And placed him across her knee.
> And with a bunch of green withy twigs
> She gave him lashes three.[87]

This unpopular face of Mary also emerges in her many apparitions over the last hundred years in which she has admonished sinners and called upon all people to live better lives.

DELIVERER: Although the doctrine of Mary as Co-Redemptrix has long been discussed, it has never been officially ratified by the Church. As the Virgin of the Annunciation, Mary assents to being the mother of Jesus, an action which is seen as redemptive on behalf of all humanity.

WEAVER: There are many apocryphal legends in which Mary demonstrates magical powers. The aspect of Weaver is well represented by the many statues of the Black Virgin throughout the world, many of which are deemed to be wonder-working.[6]

PRESERVER: Mary sustains and nourishes the natural order. Her many shrines, such as at Lourdes, testify to her continuing role of Preserver.[35]

EMPOWERER: As Virgin of the Apocalypse, Mary is depicted as clothed with the sun and with the moon under her feet. She is shown as the great Empowerer, whose wisdom is her gift, both to her son and to all living beings.

Similarly, in Hindu belief we find the concept of the Dasha-Mahavidyas, or the Ten Great Wisdoms, which likewise correspond to the aspects of the Goddess. They appear as ten wrathful or terrible aspects, forms which people in the West are unused to appreciating as positive or beneficial.

THE TEN GREAT WISDOMS (DASHA-MAHAVIDYAS)

SHAPER OF ALL: Bhunaneshvari, she who nourishes and supports all existence. She is shown as a smiling woman with breasts which ooze milk, carrying a goad and a noose.

ENERGISER: Matangi, she who has the power of domination, and who can dispel evil. She is depicted as a black woman whose eyes roll in intoxication.

MEASURER: Kali, she who has power over time. She is shown naked, with a severed head and cleaver, wearing a garland of severed heads.

PROTECTOR: Bagala, she who destroys negative forms. She is shown with a crane's head, wielding a club and pulling her enemy's tongue.

INITIATOR: Chinnamasta, she who represents the end of existence yet who distributes life-energy to all. She is shown standing upon a copulating couple, decapitating herself and feeding her attendants with her own blood.

CHALLENGER: Dhumavati, she who is the power of darkness or inertia and who gives power over these. She is shown as a widow, emaciated, ugly and quarrelsome, with a winnowing fan in her hand.

DELIVERER: Tara, she who is the gateway of re-creation. She is depicted dressed in a tiger skin with a necklace of skulls, standing upon a funeral pyre, and she is pregnant.

WEAVER: Bhairavi, she who is the active power of destruction. She has a reddish complexion, carries a rosary and a book with two of her hands and makes gestures of fearlessness and gift-bestowing with the other two. Her breasts are smeared with blood.

PRESERVER: Sodashi, she who perfects. She is shown as a nubile woman astride the prone body of Shiva and having sexual intercourse with him. They are upon a pedestal composed of the gods Brahma, Vishnu, Rudra and Indra.

31

EMPOWERER: Kamala, she who is the state of unity restored. She is shown as a beautiful woman, seated on a lotus.[49,70]

These aspects focus upon the broadest functions of the Goddess. In accordance with our prime directive, we do not have to perceive the qualities of these aspects as either good or bad – they just are. We will be examining each of these aspects through the spectrum of world mythology and spiritual tradition in more detail as this section of the book unfolds.

6. THE TEMPLE OF LIGHT

Let us return to our visualisation. As you look to the central star and its ninefold constellation, you notice that there are certain relationships between some of its satellites. These relationships are triadic, forming three equilateral triangles of great power and influence. It will be seen that each of these triads forms a composite kind of action:

- **The Transforming Triad**: transforms what the Shaper of All has made.

- **The Dynamic Triad**: energises and explores that creation.

- **The Enfolding Triad**: delimits, defines and balances that creation.

The Transforming Triad

The Transforming Triad is composed of aspect 9: The Empowerer, aspect 3: The Protector, and aspect 6: The Deliverer.

The Transformers bring about change, often in dramatic ways. The great upheavals of our lives are ruled by them, for they bring liberation. They are typified by their strength, fortitude and unchanging vision. They can be seen to represent the Goddess as Queen of

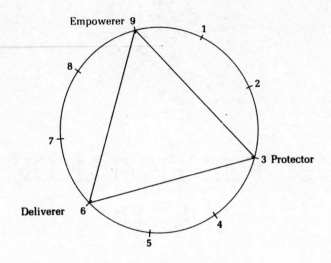

Fig. 2 The Transforming Triad

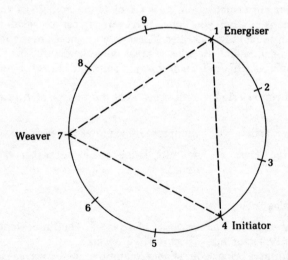

Fig. 3 The Dynamic Triad

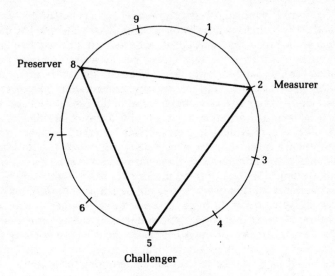

Fig. 4 The Enfolding Triad

Heaven, for they put us in touch with the supranormal dimensions of our life cycle, showing how every level of experience can be transformed.

The Dynamic Triad

The Dynamic Triad is composed of aspect 1: The Energiser, aspect 4: The Initiator, and aspect 7: The Weaver.

The Dynamics are awakeners and facilitators, each one acting as a doorway which helps us from one experience to another. They are typified by their energy, movement and ability to shapeshift. They can be seen to represent the Goddess as Queen of the Underworld, for they put us directly in touch with the ancient powers of ancestral wisdom. The Underworld within esoteric tradition is not analogous to hell as a place of suffering, but is a dimension of primal power – the real dynamo of life itself.

The Enfolding Triad

The Enfolding Triad is composed of aspect 2: The Measurer, aspect 5: The Challenger, and aspect 8: The Preserver.

The Enfolders are adjusters and rectifiers, the rulers of life. They establish the normal boundaries of our lives. They are typified by their compassion, though they may appear to be restrictive unless their lawful function is fully understood. They can be seen to represent the Goddess as Queen of the Earth, for they sustain the subtle, inter-connecting patterns of life with unswerving concentration. The earth is where our lives are lived out; the features of the Enfolding Triad are perceivable in the various and beautiful life-forms of our planet.

Another way of symbolising these triads is to think of them as octaves upon a musical instrument. In Fig. 5, we see the Goddess' Dulcimer: a lap dulcimer with three strings laid over it. Each string can be 'stopped' at one of three places to create a higher octave of the same note. In this way we will not be tempted to think of one aspect as being 'better' or more progressed than another, since each aspect resonates with its own stopped notes, as well as harmonising with the other strings. String A belongs to the triad representing the Queen of Heaven; string B belongs to the triad representing the Queen of Earth; string C belongs to the triad representing the Queen of the Underworld.

The triplicities and ninefold permutations derived from these aspects are far more subtle than arbitrary divisions of the Goddess into triple moon-phases, or as reflections of the female life cycle – Maiden,

Fig. 5 The Goddess' Dulcimer

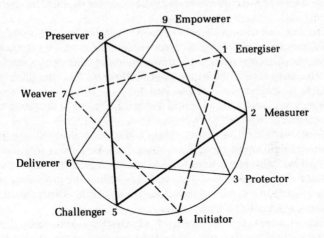

Fig. 6 The Interrelation of the Transforming, Dynamic and Enfolding
Triads

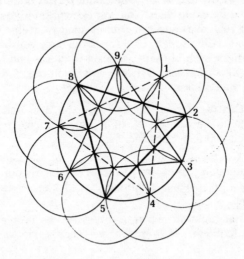

Fig. 7 The Complete Temple of Light

Mother and Crone. It is not that such definitions are invalid so much as that *each* of the triple-aspects of the Goddess contains elements of the ennead.

This ennead of aspects is endlessly adaptable for it is made up of nine, the most adjustable and yet essentially unchanging number. However one chooses to add up multiples of nine, for example 54, 72, 108, they always add up to nine. We will be studying these inter-relating triads in more detail in Part 3.

Now visualise the three sets of triads interlinked to create a powerful ennead of aspects.

Now, visualise the central star of the Shaper of All casting a great spotlight upon the ground about you. You stand in a circle of crystalline light. Now, from the heart of each aspect of the ninefold constellation, see shafts of light which fall upon the ground to create nine overlapping circles of light. These also overlap the circle of light emanating from the Shaper of All.

Each of these aspects constitute the body of the Goddess upon earth in the form of the Temple of Light. As we step into each one in the following pages, we will perhaps only be aware of its particular influences upon us, but we should remember that the same Goddess has more than just this one role, and there are many other examples which can also be used, such as how the Goddess Aphrodite functions in each of the different aspects. The best examples for you will be the ones which you have chosen and understood yourself.

Our journey will also take us through the three courts of the Temple of Light, for each of these reveals a synthesis and co-operation between the Transforming, Dynamic and Enfolding triads within the vastness of the Goddess.

The Outer Courts are where the Energiser, the Measurer and the Protector function. These are the courts of beginnings, where we find our direction and define our boundaries.

The Inner Courts are where the Initiator, the Challenger and the Deliverer function. These are the courts of instruction, where we are brought into personal relationship with the salvific stories of the Goddess.

The Courts of Light are where the Weaver, the Preserver and the Empowerer function. These are the courts of discovery and practical wisdom.

These courts are not arranged in any hierarchical way; one is not higher, better or more advanced than the others. Your journey through the Temple of Light can start anywhere, as long as you acknowledge

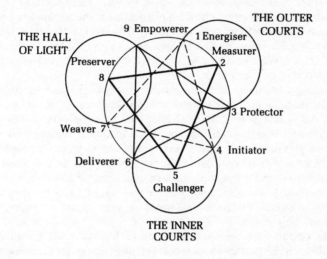

Fig. 8 The Halls within the Temple of Light

the Shaper of All first, for the Temple is dedicated to her. For the purposes of our first visit to the Temple, we will be going through each of the three courts in succession.

Like the land upon which we walk, the Temple of Light bears the features of our first mother in such a way that we may not be able to get any perspective on it at first. You can visualise it as a circular building in which one chamber leads directly to another. There are also other connections between the chambers which you may notice, but these needn't bother you yet. It may take several visits for you to orientate yourself properly, but there will be many other opportunities for you to explore it further.

LIGHT BEYOND LIGHT: SHAPER OF ALL

The little space within the heart is as great as this vast universe. The heavens and the earth are there, and the sun, and the moon, and the stars;

fire and lightning and winds are there; and all that now is and all that is not.

The Upanishads

Wherever the Goddess has manifested, she has been venerated under a multiplicity of aspects. All living traditions of the Divine Feminine acknowledge that she is one and many. This is why this book is not called The Elements of Goddesses, for modern Goddess consciousness in the West understands that the Divine Feminine principle stems from a central source.

Throughout this book, we examine myths from the many traditions of the world which have honoured the Goddess. In so doing, we must be sensitive to those traditions, for it is too easy to ransack world mythology and religion, and create 'evidence' for whatever one wishes. It is not merely expedient to rewrite history by tying together disparate traditions in order to restore the Goddess, it is misleading and disrespectful to the complex web which the Goddess has woven. It is as though we took exception to some part of a vast tapestry and started to unravel and reweave it to our own specifications, regardless of the artist's vision.

The Goddess weaves her tapestry on such a vast scale that no one can discern the pattern in its entirety. One of the major challenges of anyone desiring to encounter the Goddess is one of perspective. How shall we envisage her?

Visualise the image of the far distant star once more. To your perception it is perhaps almost insignificant compared with the immensity of space in which it seems to hang. Think of this star-jewel as the heart of the Goddess and the surrounding space as the immensity of her nature, and you will begin to comprehend how impossibly vast she really is. Before this star-jewel heart can refract any images by which we may know her, she must first be recognised as the Shaper of All. 'In the first age of the gods, existence was born from non-existence. After this the quarters of the sky were born from her who crouched with legs spread'.[86] This is none other than the Hindu Goddess Aditi, who, as primordial space, is both infinite and transcendant.

Earth hangs in space like a child in the amniotic waters of the womb. Such is the Hindu conception of primordial space which, as the Goddess Surabhi, the cosmic cow of space, provides an ocean of milk which the gods churn to provide three kinds of food: milk for human consumption, butter for ritual use and the ambrosial drink of the gods.

The nineteenth century Bengali saint, Ramakrishna, had his own vision of this aspect. He saw, emerging from the river Ganges, a beautiful pregnant woman who gave birth as she came ashore. She suckled her child. Then in an instant, the beautiful woman had became a terrifying hag who stuffed the child into her mouth and swallowed it. She then returned to the river and vanished.[78]

This startling image clearly shows the creative and catabolic actions of the Goddess. Just as the Shaper of All brings all life into being, so she reassimilates it; not in uncaring ways but according to the natural laws, for she is both giver and taker.

One of the most common images for the Goddess is of the earth itself. We shall start here, with our own living planet, for it is our home and provider in more ways than one. Within the mythologies of very many cultures, there are stories of how the Goddess formed the land, and sometimes the heavens as well, out of her own body. These are so numerous that they virtually form a creation mythology all of their own.

Creation is rarely serene and effortless. Each of us recalls the anguish of the womb-journey at some unconscious level. That same struggle to be born from the cavern of the mother's body is reflected in the chaotic geological upheaval of the earth's crust which we find in many land features the world over. The twin mountains of the Paps of Anu in Kerry, Ireland, are but one example of the way we celebrate the Goddess as landscape.

In the Babylonian creation epic, Tiamat and Apsu are the primordial couple who form the world. Tiamat is goddess of the bitter waters, just as her husband is the abyss of sweet waters. In a story which closely parallels the Greek Gaia/Cronos myth, the newly-formed gods brought to birth by Tiamat rise up and, led by Marduk, kill their father. In her attempts to kill Marduk, Tiamat gives birth to eleven monsters – similar in nature to the Greek Titans. But Marduk slays his mother, slitting her body into two so that she forms the fabric of sky and earth. Her breath becomes the clouds and her moisture the rivers of Tigris and Euphrates.[22]

Cipactli (or Tlaltecutli) the Mexican Goddess, originally existed as a monstrous alligator swimming in space. All of life was contained within her, but could not come into being until the Goddess offered up her own body. Two serpent-gods tore her into pieces, and her lower body became the earth, while her upper body became the heavens: 'From her hair they made trees, flowers, and grasses; from her skin, very fine grasses and tiny flowers; from her eyes, wells and fountains, and small caves; from her mouth, rivers and large caves; from her nose, valleys and mountains; from her shoulders,

41

mountains'.[9] Her myth was passed down to the Aztecs who fundamentally re-enacted the Goddess' sacrifice quite literally by offering her living bodies which were torn apart on her altars.[69]

The Shaper of All also creates humankind. In Greek myth, Deucalion and Pyrrha were the only righteous couple to survive the Flood sent by Zeus to destroy humankind. The couple were too old to have children and they realised that they were the last human beings alive. In despair they prayed to the Goddess, Themis, to help them. She replied, 'Depart from my temple, veil your heads, loosen the girdles of your garments and throw behind you the bones of your great mother.'[79] Puzzled, they eventually worked out that they were to cast the rocks behind them. Each stone thrown by Deucalion became a man, while each stone thrown by Pyrrha became a woman, and so the earth was repopulated.

The Romans swore their most serious oaths 'by Tellus Mater', for the earth witnessed everything and would uphold the right in every case.

Eastern veneration of the yoni (the female genital organs) may be seen in a similar light. For while 'the yoni is extolled as a sacred area, the transmission-point for subtle forces, the gateway to cosmic mysteries',[70] it is also the gateway to the reality of earthly existence. Neither the earth nor the genital organs of the Goddess can ever lie.

The many depictions in Northern Europe of the Goddess as a sheila na gig, are shown usually as a hag with genitals prominently displayed in invitation. These represent touch-stones of truthful witness, for it was the custom to touch the vulva of these statues calling upon the Shaper of All in veneration and humble acknowledgement of one's common origin.

Sibylline oracles were given from caverns within the earth where chthonic priestesses represented the voice of Mother Earth herself. Such is the sovereignty of the earth that there are few cultures who have not acknowledged a goddess of the land.

These stories present to us a major aspect of the Goddess, who creates life from her own body or, if that does not suffice, splits herself in pieces in order to create. The Shaper of All shows us the foundation mysteries of the Goddess: she who encompasses space, time and creation.

The Shaper of All asks us to consider where we feel the creative pressure arising from within us. Her birth-pangs to create the world are echoed in our own creative struggle to give birth. Unless we are willing to be broken in pieces by the effort, the result will be negligible. All artists speak of this terrible process of emergence, wherein personalities shatter in order to make room for a greater presence. This is the action of the Shaper of All.

We have to forget about trying to keep control of our lives, about our futile efforts to make life trot peacefully along the old well-worn paths. This is a prime way that serious illnesses may arise. Unless we are willing to be rent in pieces, to let go, we will find ourselves in a time and place where we spontaneously shatter because we have not had the courage to move into vastness from the narrowness of our own confines.

Finding this vastness of space grounds us in an understanding of the Shaper of All. For without this primal experience, we will never come to see how the Goddess' heart is a nine-gated crystal at whose centre She is to be found.

THE OUTER COURTS

FIRST LIGHT: THE ENERGISER

O daughters of Isis, adore the goddess, and in her name
give the call that awakens and rejoices. So shall ye be blessed
of the goddess and live with fulness of life.

The Worship of Isis
Dion Fortune

The first light of the Temple of Light is that of the Energiser. The Shaper of All brought all into existence, encompassing it within herself, while the Energiser gets life moving. Her eternal motion is the rhythm of the dance, which is why one of the symbols upon this door is the drum.

In Tibetan Buddhism, the directional dakinis exhibit this function. *Dakini* means 'sky-going woman' or 'sky-dancer'. Each of the four dakinis or *khandos*, as they are called in Tibetan, exhibits the moving energies of each of the directional elements:

DIRECTION	SANSKRIT NAME	TIBETAN NAME	QUALITY MEDIATED BY EACH
East	Dhatisvari	Dorje	Mirror-like wisdom
South	Mamaki	Rinchen	All-enriching wisdom
West	Pandaravasini	Pema	Discriminating wisdom
North	Samaytara	Lekyi	All-accomplishing wisdom

43

The directional dakinis are aspects of Vajra Varahi (Diamond Sow) who 'springs out of the cosmic cervix ... burning with unbearable bliss, (representing) energy in an unconditional state'.[2] Icons depict Vajra Varahi dancing furiously, dressed only in her ornaments and symbolic implements, with the four directional dakinis about her. The complex initiations connected with her empower students of her lineage into the spacious freedom which her energy imparts.

Rainbow light is associated with meditation on Vajra Varahi and

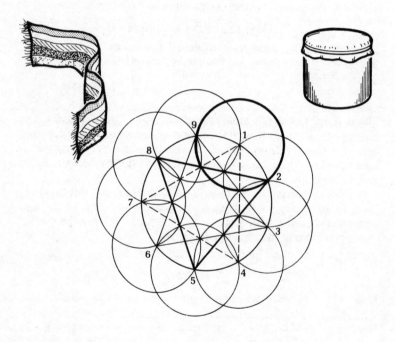

Fig. 9 The Circle of the Energiser with Her Symbols of Rainbow and Drum

her dakinis, and this is a helpful image to bear in mind when thinking of the Energiser, for she shows the complete spectrum of possibilities.[74, 94] Each of the dakinis is associated with an element. Esoterically, the four elements of air, fire, water and earth represent the bases of life. For the dakinis, as for the Energiser, each element is a channel by which life can be enhanced. Meditation upon the qualities mediated by each dakini can bring clarity to parts of the personality which are obstructed by elemental blockages or imbalances.

The unbounded Energiser is the true ecstatic. She is Aphrodite arising from the seed of Cronos who puts the whole world in the receptive state for creation. The rites of Astarte and Inanna involved the custom of nubile women offering their virginity to strangers, acting as representatives of the Goddess in a holy enactment of divine creation. In this way, all women served in the Goddess' temple before continuing with their lives. Some remained there becoming hierodules (sacred mediators of the Goddess' embraces) who never married, save on their retirement from office. It would appear that some hierodules were reluctant to retire, and loath to leave off fulfilling the office of Energiser: 'My vagina is fine, yet among my people it is said of me, "it is finished with you".'[89]

Yet while the Energiser is chiefly associated with the ecstatic act of love, she is also the one who provides the impetus for battle. Her energy can be directed anywhere. The Morrighan is famed as the triple-aspected Goddess of battle, yet she too is an ecstatic Energiser, mating with the Irish Dagda of the Tuatha de Danaan and empowering him. Her energy becomes available to the de Danaans in their battle against the Fomorian enemy.[17]

Inanna shares the same interest in matters of love and war. She is invoked as the Mistress of Heaven who commands the elements: 'You fasten combat and battle to your side; / You tie them into a girdle and let them rest.'[96] Yet she is also the one who incites to love and acts of pleasure:

> My vulva, the horn.
> The Boat of Heaven,
> Is full of eagerness like the young moon.
> My untilled land lies fallow.
>
> As for me, Inanna,
> Who will plow my vulva?
> Who will plow my high field?
> Who will plow my wet ground?[96]

Likewise, Queen Maeve of Connacht exhibits the same encompassing energy field, for she promotes battle and conflict but also sleeps with many men for her own pleasure. Her name is the chief giveaway here for, in ancient Irish, *Medbh* or Maeve means 'intoxication'.[17]

This inebriating power of the Energiser is seen in the Peyote Woman. Her devotees imbibe the peyote cactus and, in their hallucinatory visions, often hear her singing and receive songs themselves. There is an established peyote religion in the Northern American tribes whereby the non-addictive peyote is taken as a sacrament. The fact that one of the effects of taking peyote gives colour visions establishes Peyote Woman as one aspect of the Energiser, for the rainbow scarf representing all sensory experience is hers.[78]

Sometimes, the Energiser appears as the active partner of a polarised pair of deities, but she is never 'just a housewife'. In esoteric Judaism, the Shekinah herself appears as Energiser, the one who enables Yahweh to plan the creation. She gives proportion, depth and breadth of space from the vastness of her powers. As Yahweh moved on the face of the waters, it is the mirror-image of the Shekinah which appears in its depths.[63]

At other times, the Energiser appears to entice or invite union in ways which connect her to the Challenger, as when Devi creates Brahma, Vishnu and Shiva. She divides herself into three parts and promises to become the consort of each god. She instructs them to create, preserve and destroy the universe. But Shiva alone wishes to have her for his wife and he begins a programme of asceticism in order to win her. Devi then adopts several terrifying forms and appears to each one in turn. Brahma became four-faced in order to turn away from her, and Vishnu closed his eyes and plunged into the water, but she was unable to turn Shiva from his asceticism . . . 'pleased with him [she] promised to become Sati in order to marry him'.[77]

Radha appears in *The Padma Purana* as the *hladini-shakti* or blissful energy of Krishna.[78] Where many Hindu Goddesses have become submissive in later theology, Radha retains her ecstatic and even frenzied relationship with her husband, being sometimes depicted in the superior position as she and Krishna make love.

The Energiser is not beyond laughing at herself. When Demeter is mourning her lost daughter, Persephone, in the house of Metaneira, it is the antics of Baubo alone which can make her smile. Baubo, as a ribald Energiser, exposes her vulva reminding Demeter that life, not death, is the issue. Baubo's attitude is reflected by that of the sheila na gig who parts her legs to reveal all. Her image was often incorporated into the fabric of medieval churches, often placed over the door where the faithful passed in and out, so that no one might take pride in their superior condition.

The Yoruba Goddess, Oya – the dancer, the bringer of winds – appears to her worshippers in the most direct manner, for she works quite literally through her *olorisha* or priestess. Oya is a real Energiser:

> Storm wind is arriving, strong wind,
> Storm wind is arriving, strong wind.
> Oya likes a good hard lover, strong wind,
> Oya dances a wicked bamba, strong wind.[33]

The Nigerian Goddess Oshun, is likewise not averse to a 'good hard lover' either. Among a bewildering array of abilities and aspects, Oshun shows how powerful the energiser can be:

> There is no place where it is not known that
> Oshun is as powerful as a king.
> She dances and takes the crown,
> She dances without asking.[78]

Without being asked, without any effort, the Energiser excels and shows herself in both ecstatic and terrible ways.

The ecstatic nature of St Mary Magdalene comes down to us in two ways: through the Gospels, where she is combined with the woman taken in adultery, and in the Gnostic scriptures, where she appears as a true Energiser. Both pictures show the Magdalene as someone who uses the powers of the Energiser through sexual ecstasy as well as through the expansive powers of disputation and identification with the source of divine wisdom.[63]

The powerful energy of the Energiser has to be directed or it can become overwhelming. Cybele had this effect upon the priests of her cult who, in their ecstatic union with the Goddess, castrated themselves in her honour. Many see this voluntary sublimation of manhood to the Goddess as the point at which the reign of the Divine Feminine started to draw to a close, whereas up until the Classical era it had retained at least an equal footing in the mysteries. Others would see this act as right and proper reverence, but the disempowerment of any part of the Shaper of All's creation cannot be a correct use of energy. Castration, whether physical or psychic, is a denial of the life force. The ancient mysteries which sought to draw upon the vital forces of men, harnessing them to a 'higher' power by such atavistic practices – like the societies which still mutilate their men

47

and women by circumcision, sub-incision, brainwashing and so on – must pass away and be replaced by a correct observance of the Energiser's power.

The denial of the Energiser has had a terrible effect upon our society. Her dynamic powers have been much feared since they use as their points of mediation the channels of life themselves: energy and sex. The major Western myths related about the Fall revolve around figures like Eve and Pandora who bring about life. The most restrictive concept which the West has still to shake off is the delusion that the incarnation of the spirit in matter is an evil thing. The antidote for this soul-sickness is found in the Energiser and in the re-examination of the alternative myths about Eve.[81] The Gnostic scriptures give us a picture, not of a downcast, shamed Eve exiled from paradise, but a transcendent figure who gives life:

> After the day of rest, Sophia sent Zoe, her daughter, who is called 'Eve', [of Life] as an instructor to raise up Adam, in whom there was no soul, so that those he would begat might become vessels of the light. [When] Eve saw her co-likeness cast down, she pitied him, and she said, 'Adam, live! Rise up on the earth!' Immediately her word became a deed. For when Adam rose up, immediately he opened his eyes. When he saw her, he said, 'You will be called 'the mother of the living' because you are the one who gave me life.[73]

If the Shaper of All challenges us to find space within ourselves, then the Energiser gives us leave to explore that space. This is often a frightening experience for those whose own confines are narrowly straightened. The Energiser can be volcanic in her effect, demolishing the safe, cosy structures within which our lives are led. Our first encounter with the Energiser may leave us troubled and disrupted, as though a strong wind had just blown our mental furnishings everywhere. But this aspect brings us news from a forgotten country which we still have to explore. In her rainbow scarf, she breathes fresh hope and strength of purpose into lives which have become stale and profitless. She makes us explore our hidden treasures. Her motto: 'Everything to excess', pushes beyond our self-appointed limits to new freedoms.

The joy which the Energiser shows us is one which is entirely non-dualistic. She brings us to the deep places of delight, making us use parts of ourselves we had thought rusted from lack of employment. She shows us the kernel of our desire and propels it towards us with unambiguous need. When we want enlightenment, forthright and effective action, healing or whatever it is, as undualistically as we want sexual fulfilment or the appeasing of starvation by food, then we can be sure that the Energiser has been with us.

SECOND LIGHT: THE MEASURER

Our Lady is also the Moon, called of some Selene, of others Luna, but by the wise Levanah, for therein is contained the number of Her name. She is the ruler of the tides of flux and reflux.

The Worship of Isis
Dion Fortune

The Energiser brings life into what the Shaper of All has formed. Now the Measurer defines the Energiser's power, giving it fixed limits and an ordered pattern. The symbols on the door to this chamber are the wheel and the spindle.

In *The Myth of Er*, Er has a vision of the spindle of Ananke or Necessity as a great shaft of impenetrable light. The whorl of the spindle has eight circles on it, each one corresponding to the planets (including earth). Each revolving circle has its own note, making the music of the spheres. About the spindle sit the daughters of Ananke, the Fates: 'Lachesis, Clotho and Atropos; their ropes are white and their heads garlanded, and they sing to the siren's music, Lachesis of things past, Clotho of things present, Atropos of things to come'.[82] The soul draws lots from the lap of Lachesis (the measurer) and is given its Guardian Spirit before being led to Clotho (the spinner), who spins the life-thread. Lastly it comes to Atropos (the inevitable), who cuts the life-thread and the soul returns before the throne of Ananke, for the whole Spindle of Necessity lies in her lap.

This dense but explicit mythical concept shows us the nature of the Measurer. She presents the boundaries of restricted activity, yet hers is no closely confined prison, but a vast and ordered pattern of limit. The Moirae may be compared with the Norns who apportion the fate, or *weird*, of each person.

All forms must have definition. The ordered nature of the molecules in wood, for example, define for us a table or a chair, according to their disposition. We do not find fault with this kind of limitation. This is also how we must understand the Measurer. She is the mistress of defined limits and is thus also a judge and an upholder of what is right. She is also typified by images of time – the widest kind of limitation which we can conceive. Time appears

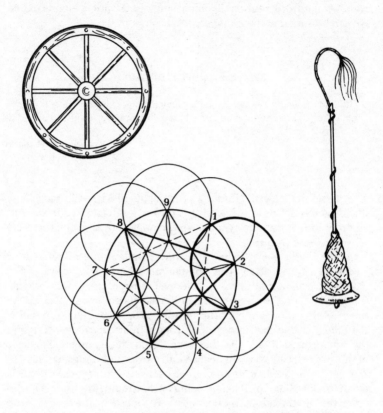

Fig. 10 *The Circle of the Measurer with Her Symbols of Wheel and Spindle*

in different ways, depending upon our motivation. Sometimes it goes too slowly, sometimes too quickly, yet time is neither good nor bad in itself.

The giant Scandinavian Goddess, Angerboda, is the mother of three delimiting offspring: Jörmungand, the giant snake; Fenrir Wolf, who would bring about the end of the world at Ragnarok; and Hel, the queen of death. These three inevitabilities are assigned their place by Odin: Jörmungand is thrown into the heavens surrounding the world of men, to encircle the earth as the Midgard Serpent; Hel is assigned the world beneath the worlds, that of Niflheim; and Fenrir is kept chained by the gods themselves, who fear the end of the world.[18] Angerboda is thus a clear aspect of the Measurer, for her offspring define the mortality of humankind, the planet and of the gods themselves.

The Greek Goddess, Themis (natural order), is likewise the mother of a series of daughters, all of whom partake of her nature: 'Bright Themis . . . bare the Horae [Hours] . . . Eunomia [Order], Diké [Justice] and blooming Eirene [Peace], who mind the works of mortal man, and the Moerae [the Fates]'.[40] Themis represents the right or natural order which binds us in everyday life. 'It is easy to obey, but it also forbids many things'.[48] Her many daughters reflect their mother's light. Hora means 'the right moment'. The Horae do not betray nor deceive; they govern the periodicities of life in accordance with the natural laws. They were the trusted guardians of the gates of Heaven and Olympus. Eunomia is really a doublet of her mother. Eirene's peace only prevails when right order and justice are upheld. One of the myths told of Diké was that, at the end of the age of silver, justice herself would forsake the earth and become exiled in the constellation of Virgo. Virgil, the Roman poet, prophesied in his fourth Eclogue that she would return to earth once more, and no time has surely needed her as much as we do now.

Diké's other, darker side was Nemesis or retribution. This face of the Measurer is also worn by the Erinyes, the angry ones, sometimes called the Furies. They were born of the blood of their father Cronos when Zeus castrated him, and their function is to visit retribution upon those who are blood-guilty. They carried torches, whips and serpents and lived in the netherworld. They appeared as avenging Goddesses to Orestes who killed his mother, Clytemnestra. In Aeschylus' play Eumenides, they are propitiated and renamed the Eumenides, the Kindly Ones, and invited to have a place of their own in the temple of Athena.

Sometimes the Measurer functions as a judge. In the Egyptian Book of the Dead, the feather of Maat is set in the scales of truth against the heart of the dead person in the hall of judgement. If the feather of truth weighs more than the heart, then that person has forfeited the mercy of the gods.

The delimiting function of the Measurer is sometimes shown in dramatic ways, as with the Irish Goddess Macha, who runs against the speediest team of horses in order to vindicate her earthly husband's boast of her speed. With her feet she traces the circuit of the place which will be called after her: Emain Macha. According to an alternative myth, she produces a cloak-pin and draws out the foundations of the city. In both instances, she dies in childbirth, leaving her curse upon the men of Ulster: that they shall suffer the weakness of a woman in childbirth for four days and five nights for nine generations, usually at the time they stand in the most need of strength. Macha shows herself as Measurer, circumscribing the fate of people yet unborn in order to balance her own sacrificial death.[59]

The Measurer is also the mistress of memory. Mnemosyne, the mother of the Muses, exercises this function in a sometimes initiatory way. She guards the waters of forgetting and remembering – the limits of memory. Those who die the first death, that of the body, drink of the waters of forgetting where the memory of the last incarnation is mercifully erased. Those who die the second death, that of initiation into the mysteries, drink of the waters of memory, where the deep memories well up to meet understanding.

The rhythmic and cyclical nature of the Measurer is nowhere better seen than in one of the major symbols of the Goddess, the moon itself, which is the mistress of the tides of growth and decay:

> I am that soundless, boundless, bitter sea.
> All tides are mine, and answer unto me.
> Tides of the airs, tides of the inner earth;
> The secret, silent tides of death and birth.
> Tides of men's souls, and dreams, and destiny.[30]

Meditation upon the moon's phases brings us into the fold of the Measurer and gives us experience of all her powers. All women already feel the circuit of the Measurer within their menstrual cycle. It prepares them for the reception of life. It brings them into the arena of physical fertility for about thirty-five years or so and then prepares them for the psychic fertility which should follow the menopause. Yet all can experience the phases of the Measurer as the moon waxes and wanes each month.

After the liberal allowances of the Energiser, we need the Measurer to help us define the limits of our new found freedom. This is not to restrict us but to safeguard our integrity, for we cannot be allowed to do just as we like. Sooner or later our excesses will result in the harming of another. The Measurer establishes her boundaries clearly so that we do not harm the rest of creation. In an age which sees all restriction as a trespass upon personal liberty, the Measurer comes to remind us of self-discipline, giving a channel for the otherwise overwhelming powers of the Energiser. The Measurer is a sure friend, often appearing in our lives as the inner guardian to remind us of our personal integrity.

The giving of destiny lies in the gift of the Measurer who apportions the outer limits of our fate, yet we need not feel 'fated' or 'doomed' for all time. The Measurer is also a renewer. She will write her runes upon the board and wipe it clean again in order to write once more. This aspect of the Goddess is particularly feared in the present ecological climate where our wilful wasting or spoiling of the earth's resources calls the Measurer into operation. As James Lovelock has written:

> Gaia . . . is no doting mother tolerant of misdemeanours, nor is she some fragile and delicate damsel in danger from brutal mankind. She is stern and tough, always keeping the world warm and comfortable for those who obey the rules, but ruthless in her destruction of those who transgress. Her unconscious goal is a planet fit for life. If humans stand in the way of this, we shall be eliminated with as little pity as would be shown by the micro-brain of an intercontinental ballistic nuclear missile in full flight to its target.[53]

This is a salutary reminder that humankind is not the ultimate species. The Measurer can wipe us out, but there is always the promise of the sibyl, the mediator of the Measurer:

> I see Earth rising a second time
> Out of the foam, fair and green;
> Down from the fells, fish to capture,
> Wings the eagle; waters flow.[4]

The purpose of the measurer is to sustain life within the established limits. It is up to us to seek her out and find our destiny; if we are true to ourselves, then we can also be true to the Measurer of our life's thread.

THIRD LIGHT: THE PROTECTOR

> Shining Beltia, exalted and most high . . .
> Have mercy on thy servant who blesses thee;
> Take his hand in need and suffering;
> In disease and distress give him life;
> May he go ever in joy and delight;
> May he tell thy prowess to the peoples of the whole world.
> Babylonian Prayer to Beltia

The Shaper of All brings everything into being, the Energiser gives power, the Measurer delimits that power: now the Protector appears to guard creation. Her symbols of bow and shield are upon this door. The Protector takes many forms but her impetus arises out of the Measurer. The Protector upholds natural law and frequently appears with forthright anger to defend her territory, but the transformative protection which this aspect affords is rooted in merciful love.

When the Hindu gods were embattled by the *asuras* (demons), they sent out their energies and evoked Durgha, one of the greatest Protectors. She fought the buffalo form of Mahishasura and each of her sighs

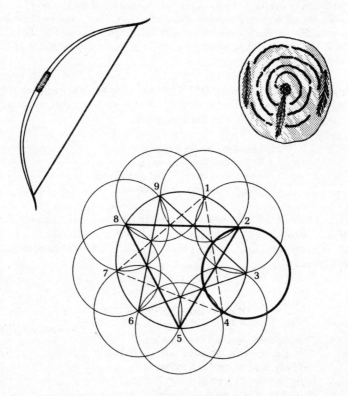

Fig. 11 *The Circle of the Protector with Her Symbols of Bow and Shield*

created a force of goddesses to combat the *asuras*. The gods revere her in these words:

> We bow before Thee, O Devi . . .
> Send us Thy thoughts for the protection of the universe
> And for the uprooting of all dangers.
> Thou whose nature is to subdue the wicked,
> Whose beauty is beyond imagining,
> Whose power destroys those who rended the devas powerless,
> Compassionate even towards those enemies . . .
> Those Thy lovely forms in the Three Worlds
> And those Thy furious forms,
> Save us in all of them.[70]

Durgha does just that. She takes on many appearances in the course of the subsequently renewed battle, including Parvati, Kaushiki and, as Ambika, becomes so angry with her opponents that the Goddess Kali emanates from her brow. An even more terrible battle ensues. The blood of the demon Raktabija spills upon the ground, creating even more combatants to fight the gods, but Kali drinks it all up, taking the energy into herself and neutralising it.

The gods make a final hymn of praise to Durgha: 'O Devi, be Thou pleased, and grant us protection from the fear of foes forever, as Thou hast protected us now by the destruction of the asuras. Destroy the sins of all the worlds and the great calamities that have arisen through the maturing of evil portents'.[70] This story shows us the possible developments of the Protector for, from her, arises also the Challenger (see page 62). The Protector assumes a variety of forms, some of which are mild and benevolent, others of which are terrifying.

Many other aspects of the Goddess go into immediate Protector mode when what they cherish is threatened. When Isis flees from the depredations of Set, she takes her son, Horus, and hides him in the marshes. She herself takes on the form of a vulture and remains thus, feeding and protecting her child until he is old enough to fight Set himself. Isis, along with many other deities, is depicted wearing the vulture skin upon her head and as a kite with out-stretched wings, is shown in the attitude of protection.

This identical theme was taken and applied to the Apocalyptic Virgin in the *Book of Revelations*, where the story of Isis and Horus is transposed to Mary and Jesus. Mary is described as: 'clothed with the sun, with moon under her feet, and on her head a crown of twelve stars; she was with child, and she cried out in her pangs of birth, in anguish for delivery'. (Revelations 12) A dragon confronts her, taking the role of Set, ready to devour the child: 'But the woman was given the two wings of the great eagle that she might fly from the serpent into the wilderness, to the place where she is to be nourished for a time, and times and half a time'. (ibid)

Sometimes the Protector takes on a terrifying form, like Dzalarhons, guardian of the earth's treasure. She sees how the people lose reverence for life by torturing in cruel games the abundant salmon which she has created. In her anger, she sends forth her punishment in the form of a volcanic eruption and pours out her fury upon the heads of the offending tribe.[69]

This reverence for what the Shaper of All made is found also in the figure of Artemis, who is in many ways her Protector. She was always depicted as a wild maiden, mostly usually with quiver, bow and hunting spear. She was born of Leto and assisted at the birth of her own twin brother, Apollo. For this, she was invoked as the patron of women in childbirth.

This is one of the Protector's prime roles: that of midwife and childhood guardian. Until her charges are old enough to fend for themselves, she watches over them, nurturing and teaching. She is sometimes the giver of arms, in which aspect she appears as Initiator.

Athene is known for being a goddess of war, but she bears no arms in time of peace and her preference seems to be to settle matters of dispute by peaceful means. She offers protection and sanctuary to the Erinnys, promising them the proper rites of hearth-altars, sacrifices, torchlight libations and first-fruit offerings. She subtly transforms the role of the Measurer and promises that any household refusing to honour the Erinnys will not prosper. In return, the Erinnys must promise to bring favourable winds for her ships, fertility and fruitfulness to fields and people, and to help her in her role of Protector by rooting out the impious. The agreement is made and Athene's city benefits. Athene is also the personal Protector of Odysseus, bringing him safely home and assisting his family.[48]

It is as a warrior, however, that the Protector is chiefly known. The Egyptian Goddess Sekhmet, known as 'the mighty one', breathes fiery vengeance against the enemies of the pharoah. She is depicted with the head of a lioness and her arrows pierce the hearts of all who come against her. She and Hathor were known as 'the Eyes of Ra', and frequently act as agents of punishment. In one legend, Sekhmet is sent by Ra to chastise humankind but once she has begun, she becomes unstoppable; it is only when the high priest of Heliopolis is instructed to grind red ochre into beer and spread seven thousand jars of it across the land, that Sekhmet halts her destruction in order to drink what she believes to be blood. Too intoxicated to continue her slaughter, Sekhmet returns and humankind is saved.[39]

Although the Protector can inflict great pain, she is also a healer. This paradoxical juxtaposition of abilities is perhaps best seen in Celtic folk-story where an old woman comes to pick up the spent body of the hero after he has achieved prodigious feats. She tends his wounds, plunging him first into a cauldron of poison in order to harden him up, then healing him in her cauldron of cure.[58] This common feature in Celtic goddesses is still clearly manifest in Brighid whose triple aspects include the patronage of smithcraft, poetry and healing.

It is thus that Sekhmet is invoked both as Queen of Battle and as Lady of Life; the one whose influence could ward off pestilence, as well as bringing it. This may have been due to the fact that the hot desert winds were thought to be her breath, which brought plague or blew it away.[55,39]

This brings us to consider the often harsh action of the Protector which, to defend creation, often obliterates part of it in the process. The Protector often works through expediency: a fact which is seen very much in our own time where our tampering with the natural law has created abnormal weather conditions in one part of the world, bringing famine, drought and sickness, while another part of the world receives a glut of fruit due to continuous good weather.

The Protector takes her cue from the Measurer and finds a measure of balance in all her actions. We think of this aspect of the Protector as 'nature red in tooth and claw', and indeed many goddesses of this aspect appear in the form of beasts, like Isis, or beast-headed like Sekhmet, or as protectors of animals, like Artemis. The Protector's anger is not like that of the Challenger which totally eradicates whatever is outworn or defunct; it is transforming anger which heals and changes.

Yet she is also a merciful Protector:

> Full are the folds of your mantle, Mary –
> (Take me to shelter, take me to hide).
> That all generations be shielded and succored,
> The cloak of their Mother is a deep cloak and wide.[35]

Even Mary, so famous for her merciful love, appears in the guise of a warrior. She is fair and terrible as an army set in array, say the scriptures. In her guise as Protector, Mary appears again in our own century to many. In an unprecedented variety of apparitions worldwide, the Blessed Virgin – to many people the only form of the Divine Feminine that they know – speaks in the warning mode of Protector: 'amend your life, open your hearts, become transformed'. The frequency and urgency of these messages, usually relayed through simple people or children, shows the world that the Protector is not idle.

The Protector enfolds us, giving us her sure hand to hold. Her heart is the fierce and tender heart of a mother whose children are threatened. As many women will testify, the first few days after childbirth bring about the most intense upheaval in a woman's life, for

Fig. 12 *The Circle of the Initiator with Her Symbols of Cauldron and Cave*

they present her squarely with the challenge of the Protector. This experience comes also to men who are new fathers. The parents of a child stand in wonderment at having helped create a baby and their protective instinct is so strong that they are shaken by the power of it. They feel the hand of the Protector upon them and, like her, are fiercely joyful and tenderly protective.

THE INNER COURTS
FOURTH LIGHT: THE INITIATOR

I have eaten from the tympanon [drum];
I have drunk from the cymbal;
I have carried the sacred dish;
I have stolen into the inner chamber.
from the Mysteries of Cybele,
as recorded by Clement of Alexandria

The Measurer sets the limits and the Protector patrols them: now the Initiator arises to set another phase in motion. Upon this door, which also gives entry to the Inner Courts of the Temple of Light, are the images of the cauldron and the cave, for the inner mysteries are enacted in this place.

The role of the Initiator is to elicit response and to explore hidden depths. This aspect always has some feature of second birth or rebirth. Within the Protector, as we saw, there is an element of reassimilation: this is fully defined in the Initiator. In some myths, this aspect often presents a kind of devouring mother – something which is frequently misunderstood. The Initiator is not like a bitch who eats her litter nor like certain aspects of the Protector which, in order to perform her function, is zealous in punishment. The Initiator has another task.

The Initiator is urgent to show the immensity of knowledge which the Shaper of All hides and, in order to do this, she is frequently shown returning people to her womb, giving them second birth. The Initiator is the guardian of the mysteries. She appears as a storyteller, a teacher, a grandmother. Being on the higher octave of the Energiser, she is a dynamic demonstrator who believes in personal, practical experience of the mysteries. It is she who puts us through the rigorous tests of our lives.

One of the prime tales of this aspect is the initiatory sequence of Ceridwen and Taliesin. Ceridwen has a son called Afagddu. She wishes to compensate him for his extreme ugliness by gifting him with knowledge, and so she brews a cauldron of inspiration for him and sets it to simmer for a year. In the meantime, she takes on an old man to stir the cauldron and a little boy, called Gwion, to fetch firewood. Towards the end of the year, some drops spill out of the cauldron and land on Gwion's finger. They are so hot, he puts his fingers in his mouth to cool them. Ceridwen is immediately aware of what has happened, and so is Gwion:

> And he saw her, and changed himself into a hare and fled. But she changed herself into a greyhound and turned on him. And he ran towards a river and became a fish. And she in the form of an otter bitch chased him under the water, until he was fain to turn himself into a bird of the air. She, as a hawk, followed him and gave him no rest in the sky. And just as she was about to stoop upon him, and he was in fear of death, he espied a heap of winnowed wheat on the floor of a barn, and he dropped among the wheat and turned himself into one of the grains. Then she transformed herself into a high-crested black hen, and went to the wheat and scratched it with her feet, and found him out and swallowed him. And, as the story says, she bore him nine months, and she was delivered of him, she could not find it in her heart to kill, by reason of his beauty. So she wrapped him in a leathern bag, and cast him into the sea.[56]

In this story, Ceridwen is both Initiator and Challenger. The fact that she brews a cauldron of inspiration and then later takes the child into her womb is significant, for we are dealing here with a mystery story. In Celtic legend, the aspect which Ceridwen fulfils is called The Dark Woman of Knowledge. It is in this guise that other faces of the Initiator come clear.

When Demeter is in mourning for her lost daughter Persephone, she wanders disconsolate to the Maiden's Well at Eleusis and there hires herself out as a children's nurse. She is led to the house of Metaneira who has recently borne a son: 'And she walked behind, distressed in her dear heart, with her head veiled and wearing a dark cloak which waved about the slender feet of the goddess.[40] Refusing a cup of wine, she mixes a special drink of barley, water and mint. (This is the *Kykeon*, and was the Sacramental drink of Eleusinian initiates.) Then she takes up her task:

> So the goddess nursed in the palace Demophoön . . . and the child grew like some immortal being, not fed with food nor nourished at the breast: for by day rich-crowned Demeter would anoint him with ambrosia as if he were the offspring of a god and breathe sweetly upon him as she held him in her bosom. But at night she would hide him like a brand in the heart of the fire, unknown to his dear parents.[40]

Metaneira discovers Demeter laying her son on the fire and makes such an outcry that Demeter is forced to reveal who she really is and that she would have made Demophoön immortal had she not been discovered. She orders the people of Eleusis to build her a temple and instructs them in the rites proper to her worship.

The very same story is told of Isis who, on hearing that the coffin of Osiris had landed at Byblus where it had been covered with heather and then taken to the king's palace to act as a pillar stone, went to the palace. She was appointed as nurse of the queen's child whom she fed with her finger rather than her breast, and in the night she burned away portions of his mortality by putting him in the fire. The queen witnessed this and cried out, depriving her child of immortality.[83] Isis bore away Osiris' coffin and subsequently Byblus, like Eleusis, became a place of special veneration.

Both Demeter and Isis perform their initiatory function for the initial benefit of one child, directly after experiencing extreme sorrow. In Demeter's case the rites of Eleusis open the initiation of the Goddess to all free-born Greeks. Ceridwen initiates only Taliesin who is reborn of her cauldron and of her womb respectively, thus receiving a second birth. In each instance we see how fire plays a great part in the narratives of the Initiator.

The Goddess Kalwadi figures largely in Australian initiation rites. The story tells how she was fond of baby-sitting but that her charges kept mysteriously disappearing. Angered at the loss of their children, the parents went in search of Kalwadi whom they found hiding in her underwater lair. Although they loved her and respected her as their Mother, the aggrieved parents slew Kalwadi and cut her open. The children, however, were not as they had supposed, in the Goddess' stomach, but in her womb awaiting rebirth.[69]

The mystical re-enactment of these stories was at the root of many ancient mystery cults. Initiation into manhood or womanhood at the traditional rites of passage is no longer a feature of Western society. In primal societies, initiates are returned to the condition of pre-childhood and are mystically reborn. Initiation into any spiritual tradition demands an approximation of these rites. Whether one is born of the waters of baptism or of the mikveh (Jewish ritual bath), a form of ritual purification similar to our original condition – that of floating in the amniotic waters of the womb – is performed.

Initiation is often painful and demanding. Even if we do not formally undergo initiatory rites, life itself confronts us with initiations which are not dissimilar. The loss and finding of the self are under the aegis of the Initiator. The karmic lessons which we have been reborn in order to learn in this incarnation have a way of recurring in our lives. We seldom know that we are working out a mythical programme – our own mystery cycle. It is a story that a part of us knows well, however, and there is no reason why we should not find the most effective method of understanding and applying its lessons rather than becoming its victim. The Initiator makes sure that our eyes and ears are open for the clues.

We also see the Initiator as foster-mother, who arms and teaches her protégés. Both Arianrhod and Athene are responsible for arming heroes with empowering weapons. Arianrhod first of all refuses to name or arm her son, and lastly refuses him permission to marry a mortal wife. Lleu's initiation is to overcome these fearsome prohibitions set by his mother and in order to do so, he must trick her into giving him both a manly name and arms without which he is a social non-entity.[56] Athene similarly bestows the gift of the reflecting shield on Perseus, which will help him to overcome the Medusa. This is a gift from the Initiator which will help the hero in his confrontation with the Challenger.[34]

The Initiator is a ruthless and thorough teacher. She is not concerned with cosseting and nurturing the initiate in cosy ways, but demands the kind of concentrated attention which a virtuoso instrumentalist expects in a class of students who have reached a standard of some proficiency. The experience of the Initiator is shocking and surprising but, like the enlivening energy of the Energiser of which she is a major harmonic, it is inspirational.

The process of initiation is rather like being let loose in a treasury full of items of power whose use you cannot know – yet. In the fullness of time, experience teaches us their significance and allows us a free rein in this treasury of possibilities so that we can live more effectively.

We enter the cave of the Initiator not only to drink of her cauldron, but also to become the mixture which she is brewing – for she teaches the way of exchange. The power so freely given to all creation by the Energiser is now returned so that others may also find Life. The melting pot of experience is thus enriched by everyone who steps into this chamber. It is only by this valid exchange – both giving and receiving power – that we are fitted to enter the next chamber, that of the Challenger.

FIFTH LIGHT: THE CHALLENGER

For Terror is Thy name,
Death is in Thy breath,
And every shaking step

Destroys a world for e'er.
Thou 'Time', the All-Destroyer!
Come, O Mother. Come!

Kali the Mother
Vivekananda

If the Initiator opens doors, then it is the Challenger who comes through them. Somehow nobody ever expects the Challenger. The symbols on this door are themselves challenging: the skull and the maze are indicative of this aspect's function, for she is mistress of the second death and is in league with the Initiator. The second death is

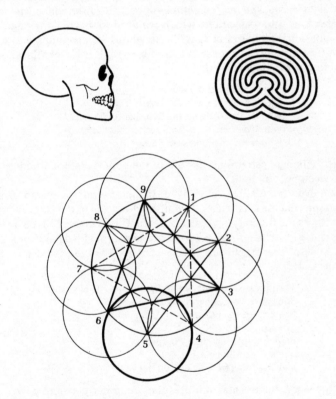

Fig. 13 The Circle of the Challenger with Her Symbols of Skull and Maze

that suffered by the initiate and, unlike the first or physical death, gives a new kind of life. The Challenger is on the higher octave of the Enfolding Triad and, like the Measurer before her, sets strict limits in the image of the maze, along whose paths all initiates must walk.

For people raised in the West, anything that opposes them is generally considered to be automatically 'bad'. In order to understand this aspect of the Goddess, we are going to have to transcend this fundamentally dualist attitude.

Both Hindu and Buddhist deities have multiform appearances, both benevolent and wrathful. In practice, of course, no one imagines that the deity in question has 'good' or 'bad' identities: the deity is an inviolate whole who may sometimes appear in guises which frighten or shock us into realisations which we need to make. For example, the blissful White Tara of long life is wholly compassionate to her devotees, but she can appear in other forms such as Kurukulla whose function is to subjugate evil:

> I pay homage to the red one,
> baring her fangs, whose body is frightful,
> who is adorned with the five signs of ferocity,
> whose necklace is half a hundred human heads,
> who is the conqueress of Mara.[8]

The Challenger certainly puts paid to the notion that the Goddess is all sweetness and light.

Not even the Mistress of Heaven, Inanna herself, is exempt from encountering the Challenger. When she descends to the Underworld to witness the funeral rites of her husband Gugulanna, she is stripped sequentially of her royal adornments and brought naked into the presence of Ereshkigal, her elder sister, who is the Mistress of the Underworld:

> Then Ereshkigal fastened on Inanna the eye of death.
> She spoke against her the word of wrath.
> She uttered against her the cry of guilt.
> She struck her.
> Inanna was turned into a corpse,
> a piece of rotting meat,
> and was hung from a hook on the wall.[98]

In this story, Inanna may not presume upon her personal power as Queen of Heaven, but has to be stripped of her symbols of office one by one until she goes naked into the Underworld. Yet, although Ereshkigal wills Inanna's death, she is herself stricken with pain and sits groaning, for she and Inanna are parts of one whole.

The Challenger is frequently depicted as the Mistress of the Underworld gates. The supreme example of this comes from Melanesia where Le-Hev-Hev challenges all who come to her land after death to play a game. She either draws on the sand in front of her complex but impartial maze or else she draws the whole maze and excises part of it, leaving it to the soul to guess the rest of the design. If the soul is successful, then it will know the route through the regions of the Underworld. If it is not, then Le-Hev-Hev dines upon it.[69]

The Challenger is not continually aggressive, but she frequently invites challenge so that what is outworn or stale can be renewed. In the Arapaho story of White Owl Woman, the Challenger appears as the season of winter which has to be overcome before spring can appear. She submits Raw Gums – a prodigious baby – to a series of ritual questions:

> 'Which travels fast?' said White Owl Woman lazily. 'It is the brain that travels swiftly and at great distance,' said Raw Gums. 'What animal is harmless to all?' . . . 'Well the most harmless creature is the rabbit.' . . . 'Which of the two hands is the most useful?' . . . 'it is the left hand, because it is harmless, pure and holy,' said Raw Gums.
>
> 'Well, grandchild, you have answered my questions readily, and so this day is a glory to you. You may now strike my head at the top', said old White Owl Woman, stooping down. Raw Gums then struck her head with a stone sledge and burst her skull, and so scattered the brains, which were the snow melting away gradually. This is why there is a season of vegetation.[9]

The Hindu Chinnamasta and the Tibetan Varjayogini is similarly depicted as decapitating herself and nourishing others with her blood. Her feet rest upon a couple engaged in sexual congress. She appears to challenge them with her raised hooked knife, but in fact she makes tantric knowledge available by her actions.[49]

Sometimes the Challenger shows ways of overcoming evil, but only if the petitioner can likewise overcome natural preferences. In this, the Challenger is the teacher of compassion, the one who asserts the truth of both the Deliverer's and the Empowerer's effect.

Stories of men encountering ugly old hags are endemic in Celtic legend. When King Arthur is challenged by a giant, Gromer Somer Joure, to discover what it is that women desire, he turns to his champion knight Sir Gawain, to help him find the answer to the riddle. He encounters a hag called Dame Ragnell who offers the solution in exchange for her marriage to Sir Gawain. Arthur agrees on his knight's behalf and Gawain, unfailingly chivalrous, accepts his unsightly bride. Gromer comes and is told the riddle's true answer, exclaiming with disgust that only his sister could have granted this solution.

Gawain is then married and left alone with his bride on their wedding night. Dame Ragnell asks him for a kiss, which Gawain gladly gives. At the moment of their embrace, Dame Ragnell turns into a beautiful woman. Brushing aside Gawain's exclamations, she tells him that he must choose either to have her fair by day and ugly at night, or ugly by day and fair at night. Unable to decide between public shame and private misery, Gawain bids her decide for herself. 'That is the answer of the riddle,' she says, 'for women desire to have sovereignty over the men they love'.[67]

Here the Celtic Cailleach (Old Woman) becomes both Challenger and Empowerer in the shape of the enchanted Dame Ragnell. She simultaneously releases Arthur from his obligation to Gromer who threatens the kingdom, and is released by Gawain from her challenging shape by the correct answer to the riddle. With the Challenger, nothing is given for nothing, but when she is unselfishly repaid, she is herself generous.

Indeed, the Challenger demands that her debts are paid. The Aztec Goddess, Tlazolteotl was considered to be the purifier of her people and only her priests could hear confessions of guilt. Since this confession to Tlazolteotl was effective only once in a lifetime, many Aztecs deferred it until the moment of death. Yet, at the point of death, there can be no deception.

The Daena is the Challenger whom the souls of the dead have to meet before they pass over the bridge either to heaven or to hell. She appears as the sum total of the person's good or bad deeds. If the soul has led a good life, the Daena is correspondingly lovely and ushers the soul over the bridge. If the soul's deeds are evils ones, then the Daena appears as a hag who drags the soul down from the bridge into hell.[63]

Just as the Measurer sets time in motion, so the Challenger withdraws time back into herself again, and gives a renewal which is both profound and surprising. With the Challenger, old patterns are restated in such a way that there is no escape from their implication. She is the guardian of the secrets of time and eternity. Whatever set of lessons one is assigned to learn in this incarnation, the Challenger restates them for us so that we can act on them in the most effective way. It is thus that the enfolding function of the Challenger is touched by the dynamic insight of the Initiator. If recurring patterns threaten to confine us in a stereotype of our true selves, the Challenger will confront us again and again saying, 'Learn this lesson well', until we are able to respond positively. She cannot be shaken off or distracted from her purpose. Those who love the Goddess come to value this aspect for her wisdom, as she leads us through pain to joyful insight. Resist her and she will dog one's footsteps to the very last.

It is better to meet with death and settle accounts before death itself comes to claim old debts. The Challenger uproots all that has reached the end of its term. She resists its continuity, for her wisdom is to renew the face of the earth and to cleanse the dark places of the heart. Her compassion is unparalleled in its effective strength.

Fig. 14 *The Circle of the Deliverer with Her Symbols of a Butterfly Emerging from a Chrysalis and a Broken Chain*

SIXTH LIGHT: THE DELIVERER

I have sunk beneath the bosom of Despoina, Queen of the Underworld;
I have passed with eager feet to the Circle desired:
And now I come a suppliant to holy Persephone,
That of her grace she receive me to the seats of the Hallowed.

> inscription found buried in the hands of an initiate
> of the Eleusinian Mysteries

The Initiator brings us deeper into the Temple of Light, while the Challenger guards the way. Now the Deliverer brings us to the heart of the Inner Courts and to the revelation that is signalled by the symbols on the door of this chamber: the butterfly emerging from a chrysalis and a broken chain.

The function of the Deliverer is to penetrate the depths of suffering and transform it. It is for this reason that she frequently takes on the burden of suffering or mortality in order to achieve this.

We have already examined one episode in the Eleusinian Mysteries, let us now look at the full story from the *Homeric Hymn to Demeter*. Persephone, the beloved child of Demeter, while out in a meadow picked a narcissus, but as she did so the earth sprang open and Hades, Lord of the Underworld, bore her away to the realms of the dead. Hecate, goddess of magic, heard her cries and with burning torch in hand, went to tell Demeter where her daughter had been taken. Demeter immediately assumed a great black cloak in her sorrow. Together they went to Helios who told them that Zeus had chosen Persephone as a wife for his brother Hades. This did not console Demeter, who came to Eleusis attired as a woman who had long been a crone, and there she came to nurse Demophoön. When the baby's mother exclaimed at the manner in which the nurse was treating her child, Demeter immediately resumed her goddessly beauty. After commanding the people of Eleusis to build her a temple, Demeter caused a deadly year to pass for humankind: the seasons came to a halt, the growing season never came.

At the request of humankind's importunate prayers, Zeus permitted Demeter a sight of Persephone with the proviso that her daughter should not have eaten while in the Underworld. But Hades had given Persephone a pomegranate of which she had eaten, and so the length of time that she could remain with her mother each year was dictated by the number of seeds within the pomegranate. The joy of Demeter and Persephone being reunited was augmented by Hecate, who also embraced the returning maiden, becoming her servant and companion from that time on. Demeter instructed the guardians of her temple at

Eleusis in her mysteries and the earth was once more restored to fruitfulness.[40]

This simple story has complex layers to it. Although it is Persephone who descends to the Underworld, the role of Deliverer is fulfilled by Demeter and Hecate as well as by Persephone. The three goddesses form, to some extent, a composite group with Demeter and Persephone jointly fulfilling the main role of Deliverer and Hecate in the role of the Weaver. Yet both Demeter and Persephone take on the appearance which is normally associated with Hecate, the weaver and enchantress, for Persephone descends into the Underworld for the long enforced separation from her mother where she becomes the Mistress of the Dead. (In this role, she was also called Despoina, the Mistress.) Demeter also undergoes a Hecate-like change from a deep-bosomed goddess with plaits like ears of corn to a haggard crone consumed by grief.

The descent of Persephone and her joyous return was the subject of the Eleusinian Mysteries where the worshippers celebrated and personally re-enacted the three phases of the Deliverer for themselves. They carried torches to light the way like Hecate, suffered through fasting and purification like Demeter, and finally experienced the resurrection of Persephone from the realms of the dead. In the long course of the Eleusinian Mysteries not one initiate divulged the secret rites which Demeter had inaugurated, though some wrote of them in veiled language: 'Thrice happy are those mortals, who having seen those rites, depart for Hades; for to them alone is granted to have a true life there. For the rest, all there is evil'.[38]

So wrote Sophocles about the Eleusinian Mysteries. The Deliverer, if we are to credit his words, liberates the soul from the horrors of physical death. The fact that Persephone remains in the Underworld for part of the year is not a failure of the Deliverer's purpose, but its fulfilment, for every one of her initiates can turn to Demeter while they live, or to Persephone when they die, while Hecate will ever light the ways between with her flaming torch.

It is the way of the Deliverer to explore fully the nature of sacrifice. This is a much misinterpreted word, for it bears implications of blood-offering and of bitterly giving up what is precious. Our normal use of the word omits its vital and essential meaning which is of 'making sacred'. The Deliverer makes all things sacred or holy; she makes them whole, reconnecting them to their sacred purpose. There is often a great deal of masochistic sentimentality surrounding the transformative actions of the Deliverer. This can be witnessed from the development of the same role in Christianity where Christ himself appears as Saviour, and endless icons of the Crucifixion and images of devotion to his sorrowing mother abound. This is not to belittle the action of any delivering deity, for these imbalances arise from the devotee's incorrect alignment with the principle of delivering transformation rather than from the deity itself. However, the intrinsic symbolism of Christianity has tended to lead to a glorification of suffering in some quarters. This legacy is still with us.

The Deliverer does not promote needless suffering although she often undergoes great torments, taking on the suffering of others and transforming it by her corresponding capacity for compassion. There is nothing virtuous or glorious about suffering: it does not necessarily make us into better people unless we can find our own capacity for compassion. The egos of some people are certainly enhanced by suffering: they *become* their illness and are unwilling to be cured because of the status or attention they derive from it. The Deliverer cuts through such self-deception.

The manner in which the Sumerian Goddess Inanna descends to the Underworld and is hung on a hook like rotting meat may seem like a travesty of deliverance, but it bears comparison with the Tibetan practice of the *Chöd*. The mistress of this traditional practice is Machig Lapdron, whose study of the *Prajna Paramita Sutra* (the Discourse of Transcendental Wisdom) taught her that there is no self-essence, that a separate ego is nonsense. Practitioners of the Chöd follow the example of Machig Lapdron and literally offer up their bodies. They visualise consciousness leaving them and transforming itself into a wrathful dakini who then chops up the body, transforming its essences into a nectar which is then offered to all kinds of beings.[2] This extraordinary visual practice is an opening and offering of what we normally perceive to be our selfhood. It transcends personal identity by transforming the physical body into nourishment for the whole of creation. The wrathful dakini with her hooked knife effects this transformation leaving the body in pieces, in just the same way that Inanna is treated.

Sometimes the Deliverer chooses mortality in a very specific way. There are many heroines of legend who may be considered in this guise. They are women in whom the Goddess has taken root and made her home. Sometimes the Goddess herself takes on mortality.

Rhiannon is betrothed to Gwawl in her Underworld home, but she chooses instead to become a mortal woman and actively selects Pwyll as her mate. She bears a son which is stolen the same evening by the agents of Gwawl and, to justify their lack of attention, the midwives pretend that Rhiannon killed and ate her own son. Although

Rhiannon begs them to tell the truth, they persist in these slanders and it is judged that the Queen of Dyfed shall stand at the mounting block near the gates, and there tell all who come that way of her crime, offering to bear them into the hall on her back like a horse. She has to endure this punishment for seven years until her son, who has been rescued and raised by Teyrnon, comes to court to liberate his mother by his simple presence.[56,61]

The great tantric mistress, Yeshe Tsogyel achieves a great deliverance on all levels of her existence through concentrated spiritual discipline to such an extent that she becomes an accomplished dakini, capable of empowering, healing and teaching many. One incident in which she was raped, gives much fruit for the many victims of assault in our own time. Yeshe, always one to transform every action, even makes rape a positive experience. 'If a woman's rapists can be led to a profound recognition of their existential reality through the experience a woman gives them, there is no situation whatever that cannot be turned to advantage on the path.'[21] Her attackers are spiritually enlightened as soon as they have contact with her and their act of violence becomes transformed into an initiation. She is able to pacify and destroy their violence, and to enrich and direct their spirituality.

The Shekinah of Jewish tradition was the co-creator with Yahweh of the whole world. According to an early third century Babylonian Amora (scriptural commentary) and to subsequent Qabalistic tradition, the Shekinah voluntarily left paradise in order to be among her people. This happened either from the point when Adam and Eve were expelled from paradise, or else when the Israelites built the Tabernacle: 'On that day a thing came about which had never existed since the creation of the world. From the creation of the world and up to that hour the Shekinah had never dwelt among the lower beings. But from the time that the Tabernacle was erected, she did dwell among them'.[80]

However, when the Israelites stopped their wandering in the desert, the Tabernacle was housed in the temple erected by Solomon in Jerusalem, where the Shekinah was believed to have her home. That was destroyed twice: once in the Babylonian exile and once again under the Roman occupation. Many devout Jews after the Diaspora studied to become worthy homes for the residence of the Shekinah, who was believed to be without a dwelling since the temple's destruction. The special relationship which the devout had with the Shekinah brought them deliverance from exile, giving them access to the holy state, once available only in paradise.

The way of the Deliverer is that of bondage-breaker. Whatever is trapped, denied freedom or movement, the Deliverer personally sets free. Her method of liberation is to go to the roots of the blockage and literally blast it free. In this, the Deliverer bears a strong resemblance to the Shaper of All, who is willing to be broken into pieces.

The symbolic image of this transformation is that of the butterfly emerging from the chrysalis: from apparent death and destruction arises a new form of life. So are we borne of the Deliverer, reshaped and transformed to live more effectively within our chosen field of operation.

The Deliverer is a strong ally for all who feel victimised by life, for she shows the delusion of self-cherishing and opens up the mysteries of compassionate regard for all creation. No experience is so dreadful that we cannot find the compassion of the Deliverer within us. It is that compassion which breaks our bondage to fear. In the current climate of emerging feminine consciousness there is great need of the Deliverer. When women have gone through the initial stages of anger and recrimination, the compassion of the Deliverer is essential if they are not going to replay the pattern of eternal victims.

The Deliverer literally breaks the chain which we unthinkingly pass on to others. That chain is forged of misery, disappointment, frustration and despair, all energies which we unwittingly project onto others, making them fellow slaves of our obsessive and self-deluded cares. The Deliverer says, 'the chain is broken here, irrevocably; let there be a new beginning'. Her sacrifice is vast enough to enable us to share in the transformation of spirit which she brings. As the higher octave of the Protector, she is our ultimate guardian and wayshower for, from the heights of heaven to the depths of our desperation, there is no place where she is not.

We have come through the Inner Courts to the heart of the Temple of Light. Let us turn now to the Courts of Light and discover the broad path which leads outwards again.

THE COURTS OF LIGHT
SEVENTH LIGHT: THE WEAVER

But there was the house of the Goddess, and there they stood in the gate,
And Circe heard they singing in a lovely voice within,
As she wove on the web undying, such works as the God-folk win,
Such works as are all-glorious, and delicate and fair.

Homer, translated by William Morris
The Odyssey

The Courts of Light show us another triad of functions where the Goddess works to give us the means to continue our life.

The doorkeeper of the Seventh Light is the Weaver. The Weaver has been called Sorceress, Enchantress and Witch, but we will call her Weaver for that is her special art. Her two symbols are the spider's web and the mask. Like a spider she can weave webs across this door or else put into our hands the guiding thread which will lead us out of the crystalline labyrinth of the Temple.

This is how Hecate leads Demeter to Persephone, a role imitated by countless initiates of the Eleusinian Mysteries who bore their torches

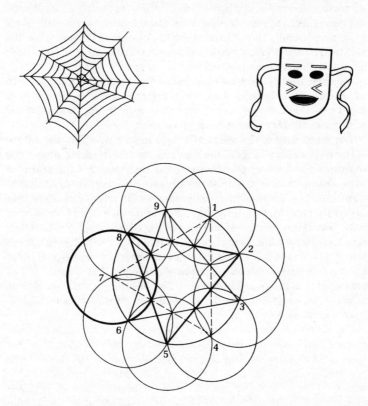

Fig. 15 *The Circle of the Weaver with Her Symbols of Web and Mask*

down the sacred way to re-enact the holy rites. Hecate is found at a crossroads, under a waning moon with dogs howling their lovesick song. She is the giver of gifts: 'For to this day, whenever any one of men on earth offers rich sacrifices and prays for favour according to custom, he calls upon Hecate ... [Zeus] did her no wrong nor took anything away of all that was her portion among the former Titan gods; but she holds, as the division was at the first from the beginning, privilege both in earth, and in heaven, and in sea.'[40]

The Weaver is also a disguiser, which is why a mask appears on the door of this chamber. Hecate appears with three heads: a serpent, a horse and a dog. When Circe invokes Hecate in the *Metamorphoses*, the stones begin to rumble, dogs bark and the earth crawls with black snakes, so potently does Circe invoke the Weaver.[79] Circe also has the ability to transform men into the shapes of wild beasts, as Ulysses and his companions discover.[34]

We have already seen an example of this shape-shifting ability in Ceridwen who combines the roles of Initiator and Weaver (see page 59). There she does not disdain from taking the shape of any animal of earth, sea or air in her pursuit of Taliesin.

The mutability of the Weaver is held to be suspect by the values of the physical world. Like the Energiser whose dynamic power she shares and enhances, the Weaver calls into question the realm of appearances. She is the mistress of changing worlds and is often shown in the guise of a faery woman who entices mortals into unearthly regions, beguiling and enchanting them. Only those who have passed through the experience of her sister aspect, the Initiator, may travel with impunity. Those who, like Thomas the Rhymer, pass into the realms of faery, find that they return to a world grown older but they themselves have acquired the 'tongue that cannot lie', or the gift of true prophecy and vision. The Weaver grants such gifts as music, poetry or healing to her favourites in return for their magical companionship.

The Weaver seems to be exempt from any attempt to subsume her powers. We have seen how Zeus was unable to strip Hecate of her ancestral Titanic powers. A similar theme appears in the story of Isis. She sends a poisonous snake to bite Ra, the highest of the gods. In his weakness, he calls Isis to heal him, but she pretends to be powerless to overcome the wound unless she knows Ra's secret name. As this contained his essential power Isis was able to restore him to health and knowledge of his secret name gave her the upper hand.[37]

This ability to gain and wield power is not surprising, for the Weaver is one of the Dynamic triad (see page 72) and *dymanis* means power. The Weaver's use of power has much to teach us about our own mortal potential, for we are always on the look out for magical powers or a cosmic 'pay-off' which will grant us empowerment. The Weaver teaches us that this is delusion, as in the following story.

The Brule Sioux tell how a snake-like monster called Unecegila once roamed about. Whoever killed it and removed its crystal heart would have great powers of prescience, persuasion and providing. It could only be killed if someone shot it in the seventh spot behind its head, but whoever looked upon Unecegila would die and so would the rest of his family.

Two twin brothers decided to attempt this feat. The younger was blind and so would be invulnerable to Unecegila. But how, then would he shoot the monster? The brothers went to petition Old Ugly Woman for her magical arrows which never failed their targets. Old Ugly Woman saw that they were poor and so she demanded that one of them sleep with her. The older brother refused since she was so ugly, but the blind brother consented and she immediately became Young Pretty Woman. She made the arrows and prophesied that the blind brother would see again, at which point he should return to her.

The boys successfully shot Unecegila and were careful to ignore the pleadings of Unecegila's crystal heart to perform certain actions which would restore it to life. With blood from the monster, the blind brother restored his sight. They kept the crystal heart and listened to its advice: It gave them great powers so that they both became important chiefs. However, the exercise of power became burdensome to them, for they always hit their target, always knew the future and always found pretty women. Then they remembered that Young Pretty Woman had told them that if the crystal heart was seen by anyone other than themselves, they would lose their powers. So they invited everyone into the tepee where the crystal heart was lodged, and it flew into many pieces, thus dispersing the power. The responsibility for wielding its power immediately fell off the brothers' shoulders and they took up their ordinary lives once more.[9]

Both Unecegila and Old Ugly Woman act in the roles of both Challenger and Weaver in this story. Unecegila is a source of immeasurable power but the sight of her kills. Old Ugly Woman helps the brothers achieve power but one of them has to lie with her against his natural inclinations. They learn that total power is both addictive and dissatisfying – a message that Old Ugly Woman tries to tell them. The Weaver measures herself against their response and they are found wanting, until they find the freedom which comes from 'giving up' power. The implication in the story is that personal application of power corrupts, but the sharing of power for the good of the tribe benefits all.

In Isis we see a combination of the abilities to weave magic and to heal, a facility which is accorded to all witches. A sixteenth century BC papyrus addresses the following prayer to her: 'O Isis, thou great Mage, heal me, release me from all things that are bad and evil and that belong to Seth, from the demonic fatal sicknesses – as thou hast saved and freed thy son Horus'.[97]

Isis, like Ceridwen, is an alchemist. She is called 'Mistress of the Perfect Black'. This expression arises out of the word for Egypt which is 'the Land of the Black or Fertile Soil'. It also refers to the blackness of the *prima materia* – the primal substance from which the final gold is transmuted. The Goddess went to the Temple of Hormanouthi and was there given the science of alchemy.[52] This is perhaps referred to in Plutarch's note about the robes of Isis: 'those of Isis are variegated in their colours; for her power is concerned with matter which becomes everything and receives everything, light and darkness, day and night, fire and water, life and death, beginning and end'.[83] Before the black stone can become gold, it passes through a variety of colours, called in alchemy 'the peacock's tail'. The many coloured cloak of Isis weaves and covers the whole of life.

The Weaver certainly inspires fear in the form of Tlazolteotl, however, when she appears as the archetypal witch. In her four aspects she rode a broomstick through the night, attired in a tall pointed hat, and frequented crossroads. Here many important decisions were debated.[69] But this aspect of the Weaver as Enchantress is really much deeper. With the Initiator, the Weaver guards the mysteries and reweaves the patterns which we create in our lives. What we consider as enchantment is usually self-delusion, a self-created paranoia in which the Goddess as enchantress has been the object of our projections and made to carry the burden of our problems.

The Weaver restates the wild energies of the Energiser and draws upon the mysteries of the Initiator to weave her vision. She is so near to the mysteries of life and death that she can operate as healer, sibyl, alchemist or dakini. Those who fear their proximity to mortality call upon her for aid but usually reject the Weaver as a witch when challenged. The Weaver is the confidante of therapeutic skills, the mistress of dreams and their interpretation, the tarot-reader, the gipsy queen. She is the go-between or midwife who sees us into or out of being. Those who work esoterically know that she is to be surely trusted as a skilled facilitator between this world and the Otherworld, one who has no desire to deceive the true traveller, but one who will lead the dilettante a merry dance, masking and disguising as she goes.

The Egyptian Goddess Neith was called 'the Opener of the Ways' and was considered a kind of female Anubis, conducting the way into the Underworld. Her symbol of an arrow was latterly replaced by a weaver's shuttle and she was known as a magician and arbitrator between Horus and Set. Her temple at Sais was famed for its inscription: 'I am all that has been, that is, and that shall be. No mortal has yet been able to lift the veil which covers me'.[22]

Ariadne is priestess of the Weaver, giving into the hands of Theseus the red thread which leads him in and out of the labyrinth. We see how the Initiator and the Energiser are subsumed into the aspect of the Weaver, who both enlivens, initiates and unfolds the mysteries.

Before Eve was mother of all living things, Adam was married to Lilith. She was the mother of a brood of titanic children whose powers were not like those of mortal kind. While later Semitic tradition has represented Lilith as the queen of demons, she may rather more aptly be called the original mother of daimons.[80] The *daimon* was the indwelling spirit or genius of each soul whose motivational help inspired mortals. In its original meaning, daimon has no connotation of malicious intent.

Those who court the Weaver come to the heart of the mysteries of creative life, for she is the supreme alchemist and artist, a many-skilled mistress of magic. These powers are not to be feared, save by those who are not grounded in reality – an experience which the Preserver very willingly supplies.

It is thus that the Weaver stands at the door of the Courts of Light, concealing and disguising the mystery of the Goddess from the profane, until the last veil between the Goddess and ourselves is rent by understanding.

EIGHTH LIGHT: THE PRESERVER

As a clear and untilled space thou madest the divine Ear of Corn to burst forth; hail, thou living Table having space for the Bread of Life; hail, Lady, perennial fountain of living water.

Akathist Hymn

The Weaver is involved in teasing out new ways for life to develop. Now the Preserver appears to maintain and nourish life. At first, it may seem that the Preserver and the Shaper of All are one and the same, but this is not so. The Shaper of All is responsible for creation; the function of the Preserver is to maintain that existence. The prime symbols of her function are the hearth fire and the grain jar, and these are shown on the doorway.

The Preserver may seem to be ill-adapted to sit beside such aspects as the Measurer and Challenger, yet she is their highest octave. The Measurer establishes the limits of reality, the Challenger patrols those limits, but the Preserver truly inhabits them, breathing into them the breath of her sustaining life.

The earliest stories about the Preserver show very proper concern for bodily nourishment. The Japanese Goddess, Ukemochi, literally meaning 'food producing goddess', provides food by vomiting. Facing the land, she vomits rice; facing the sea, she vomits fish; facing the

Fig. 16 *The Circle of the Preserver with Her Symbols of Grain Jar and Hearth Fire*

mountains, she vomits game. Rather like the Shaper of All, Ukemochi forms food from parts of her body rather than from the land:

> From her head the ox and horse; from her forehead, millet; from her eyebrows, silkworms; in her eyes, panic grass; in her belly, rice; in her genitals, wheat and beans. These commodities are taken up by the messengers and shown to the Sun-Goddess. Whereupon Amaterasu makes seeds of the grain and appoints a divinity to sow them for the future sustenance of mankind. Moreover, placing the silkworms in her mouth, she reels thread from them and thus found the art of silkworm culture.[23]

Isis likewise says of herself, 'I was the first to reveal to mortals the mysteries of wheat and corn'.[22] Indeed, without the grains of the world – wheat, corn, maize, rice and so on – humankind would have to hunt to stay alive.

The Pueblo Indians were barely able to live on the sparse grasses that grew where they lived, so they made an offering of the most brightly coloured grass seeds that they had, and built a great fire in honour of the Sun who sent down six sisters, the Corn Maidens. The sisters danced among the grasses and transformed them into different coloured corn.

After a while the people grew disrespectful of the corn, knowing that the Corn Maidens' dance brought abundant crops, and they began to rip the ears off and leave them lying about on the ground. The Corn Maidens then hid in the land of the Katchinas and the people, at last brought to famine, were sorry for their actions and begged the Corn Maidens to return. Eventually, the God of the Dawn, Paiyatuma, played his flute and encouraged the sisters to return. They came with seed corn of six colours – yellow, blue, red, white, speckled and black – and the people were taught to take care of the fields and have respect for the flute music of Paiyatuma. They learnt to enact the mysteries of the corn choosing people to represent the Corn Sisters and the Dawn God.[100]

Corn is considered to be so sacred among the Pueblo Indians that a full cob of corn, intricately decorated, is laid on the altar during ceremonies. Cornmeal is also used ceremonially to anoint priests and sacred objects, and is sprinkled on the ground to make a sacred pathway to the kiva (sacred underground enclosure). It is sprinkled also on newborn children and on the fields to impart blessing.

Throughout the agricultural world, the many rituals of harvest and sowing reflect the nature of the Preserver. We have already seen how Demeter and Persephone perform much the same function by inaugurating the Eleusinian Mysteries which are, at one level, the seeding of the earth and at another, the fructification of the spirit. Ovid describes the rites of Ceres and the merrymaking of harvest:

> Three times round the freshly bladed corn
> The blessed victim guide, while all the choir
> In gladsome company an anthem sing,
> Bidding the Goddess to their lowly doors.
> And let no reaper touch the ripened corn
> With sickle keen until his brows bind
> With twine of oak-leaf, while he trips along
> In artless dance with songs in Ceres' praise.[7]

While the harvest brings good cheer, rites of propitiation are also required. The reciprocal hunger of humankind and the fields was sometimes enacted in sacrificial rites.

Nerthus was drawn upon a cart throughout the land, blessing it wherever she went. During the time the ritual procession circuited the land, peace prevailed. When she returned to her sacred grove her cart was ceremonially washed by slaves who were afterwards drowned.[93] It is difficult to understand such rites in the light of our relatively plentiful supply of food, but for people who lived purely off the land, hard times brought hard remedies.

The Preserver, however, does not need sacrifice for she is bountiful according to our balanced use and observation of nature. She is one of the Enfolding Triad and thus cannot be pushed beyond her limits. Overproduction of the land brings barrenness. Overuse of fertilisers and pesticides creates dead soil. There is no room for complacency with the Preserver.

Mary is herself the focus of the Preserver. Medieval European legend tells of her escape from Herod into Egypt with Jesus and Joseph. As they pass through a field, hotly pursued, grain grows up from the prints of their feet and hides them: 'Then there came through the ploughland the men of Herod of heathen worship; though it was sudden, folk were reaping it throughout the crop of the ploughland all at once.[7] In the act of preserving the life of her son, Mary also gives life to the fields and nourishment to the people who help conceal her.

Creation does not live by bread alone, however. The re-creation of life is also the province of the Preserver. Joy and pleasure are hers, as well as the many arts of life. When Hathor quarrelled with Ra, her father, Thoth was deputed to persuade her to come back: 'Without you, the temples are empty and silent. Without you there is no music or dancing, no laughter or drunkenness. Without you, young and old despair, but if you come back with me now harps and tambourines, lutes and cymbals will sound again. Egypt will dance, Egypt will sing, the Two Lands will rejoice as never before.[37]

Prime among Hathor's many aspects is this ability to give joy. Yet she also continues to act as Preserver in the Afterworld where, as Lady of the Sycamore, she sometimes embodies herself as or hides within a sycamore tree and appears to the soul of the departed with fruit, and the bread and water of welcome. By partaking of these, the soul becomes the guest of the Goddess and acknowledges her guidance and help.

The river Sarasvati in northern India is the physical embodiment of the Goddess Sarasvati. Her bountiful waters bring fertility to the dry regions and, 'like Soma, she pervades creation'.[49] (Soma is believed to be the ambrosial essence of the gods.) She is depicted with her *vina*, symbolic of her patronage to the full range of arts and sciences which gladden the hearts of all.

The Greek Mnemosyne, the mother of the Muses, may also be considered in the light of the Preserver, for she guards the wells of memory.

Perhaps the best all-round example of the Preserver is found in Brighid, who is known as the patron of poets, smithwork and healing. She is the preserver of tradition for, in Celtic countries, poetry is a sacred task which transcends mere versifying. There, poets are the embodiment of ancestral memory. The ability to work with metals underpinned the whole of Celtic culture, and smithwork was considered to be a magical profession. The druidic mysteries of healing were also under Brighid's aegis, as the widespread network of Bride's wells testifies throughout the British Isles. Some of these wells preserve traditions of healing qualities, and the nearby thorn trees are usually bedecked with 'clooties', or cloth rags which suppliants tie in the branches in token of their sickness. Brighid became subsumed into St Brigit of Kildare, one of whose symbols was the cow of plenty, and in many legends we read about her miraculous provision of ale, dairy products or fish.

Brighid was ceremonially acknowledged as the keeper of the domestic hearth in Gaelic Scotland:

> I will raise the hearth fire
> As Mary would.
> The encirclement of Bride and of Mary
> On the fire, and on the floor,
> And on the household all.[13]

A similar chant is made at the end of the day when the fire is extinguished or subdued. The woman of the house rakes the embers into a circle and divides them into three separate sections with a small boss in the middle. Then three lots of peat are placed in the spaces and ashes scattered over all of it so that the fire is banked down safely for the night but can easily be reanimated in the morning.

The original sanctuary of St Brigit at Kildare kept a perpetual fire burning in honour of the saint, each nun taking her turn to watch the fire and on the turn of the last, nineteenth nun, she was to say, 'Brigid guard your fire. This is your night'.[31] The Gaelic ritual of smooring the hearth may well be a remnant of this ancient custom which was discontinued during the Reformation.

The Greek Goddess, Hestia, like Brighid, was an essential part of the home. She was never depicted in statues but was considered to be present in the fire. A new home was not considered truly founded until the woman of the house had brought fire from her mother's hearth to light the new hearth. This custom was preserved by Greek colonists who brought fire from the public hearth of the foundation mother city to establish new hearths. Hestia was the first-born of the Olympian gods and the proverb, 'Begin with Hestia' testifies to the importance placed in her as the Preserver.

The acts of the Preserver are the familiar domestic actions of daily life which, because of their familiarity, we tend to despise or overlook:

> The simplest actions should be done with a full realization of their significance, giving them an opportunity to communicate their elemental meaning in our lives – pouring water from a jug, kneading bread, breaking an egg, observing the unconscious movements of those we love, working the earth, paring vegetables, singing a song . . . Through them God our Mother communicates with us through her body, within her own mysterious creation . . . We are physically signed with the earth symbols of the divine Generatrix.[15]

By caring for these unconsidered daily actions which punctuate our lives so frequently, we find communion with the Preserver, thus becoming preservers ourselves. She gives a grounding in reality which none who seek to venerate the Goddess can ever despise. Whoever cannot sit beside the fire as part of the human family and share a meal with everyone already seated there has no part in the circle of the Preserver, but for those who love the Goddess, she makes our every action upon earth a sacrament wherein the whole of creation is enfolded.

NINTH LIGHT: THE EMPOWERER

> I am the knowledge of my inquiry,
> and the finding of those who seek after me,
> and the command of the powers in my knowledge
> of the angels who have been sent at my word,
> and of gods in their seasons by my counsel,
> and of spirits of every man who exists with me,
> and of women who dwell within me.
>
> From the Gnostic Text,
> *The Thunder, Perfect Mind*[73]

The Weaver spreads her spider's web and the Preserver provides nourishment. Now, the Empowerer bestows wisdom. The symbols upon this door are hard to discern for they can be as various as there are forms of wisdom. Two such symbols for the Western world are the mirror and the pipe of peace, though you may know others which are nearer to your heart.

The Empowerer includes the aspects of both Protector and Deliverer within herself, and is, in fact, their higher octave. The Protector is the guardian of the youthful, uninitiated person. The Deliverer is the way-shower of the initiate who knows the story of the Goddess. The Empowerer gives true maturity to all, making us 'streetwise' as we go about the world.

In every country, in every time cycle, there is one particular form of the Goddess who enjoys supreme honour. Whether she be Isis, Kwan Yin, Tara or Mary, she enjoys universal credit for accomplishing great changes. This is one of the features of the Empowerer, so strong is her focus that she subsumes many of the aspects under her aegis.

Empowerment is about giving the power which will help us take effective action in our lives. It is also a two-way process. When we have been personally empowered, then we are able to empower others. But in order to receive empowerment we have to be of one heart with our teacher. If there is any sense of being patronised or if the student holds the teacher in low esteem, then the knowledge which is the kernel of that empowerment cannot take root. Similarly, it cannot be transmitted on a solely intellectual level. Empowerment sinks through all layers of being, affecting them all.

Throughout the world, all forms of the Empowerer are at the forefront of popular veneration. Very simple and unsophisticated people are likely to obtain empowerment from the Goddess because they

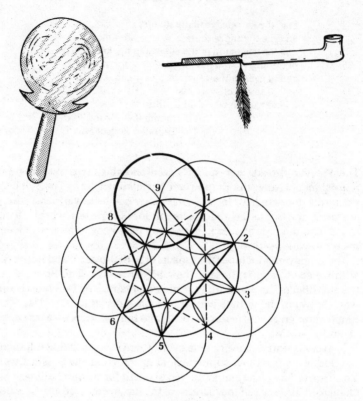

Fig. 17 *The Circle of the Empowerer with Her Symbols of Mirror and Pipe of Peace*

know instinctively that to go for help to the Empowerer is to get to the heart of wisdom. One of the true signs of the Empowerer is the fact that she is not distinguished chiefly for her myths, but for her ongoing deeds. The major Empowerers of East and West demonstrate this clearly:

> True Kuan Yin! Pure Kuan Yin!
> Immeasurably wise Kuan Yin!
> Merciful and filled with pity,
> Ever longed-for and revered!

> O Radiance spotless and efful-
> gent!
> O night-dispelling Sun of Wis-
> dom!
> O Vanquisher of storm and flame!
> Your glory fills the world.[11]

Kwan Yin is called, 'Hearer of Cries' and her power can be invoked by anyone at all. She represents the beneficent mind which enables the skilful channelling of power to her suppliants. Kwan Yin's image, like that of her Tibetan counterpart Tara, once appeared in almost every Chinese home.

Tara is likewise honoured by all Tibetans who have many detailed visualisations which accompany her veneration:

> You are adorned with the finest garments
> and many precious gems,
> your gift-bestowing right hand
> grants magical attainment to him who evokes you,
> your left hand grasps a lotus flower,
> symbol of your stainless purity,
> your two hands
> are the union of Means and Wisdom:
> boundless body of union
> I pay homage to you.[8]

In the West, two other manifestations of the Empowerer, Isis and Mary, are similarly linked in lineage, for as we have seen, Mary shares many mythic links with Isis.

The Empowerer is also seen to be a channel or bridge of wisdom, sometimes of her transcendent self, sometimes of a greater power. In the case of Mary the gifts of the Divine Feminine are included with those of the Divine Masculine:

> What joys are fountained for the world
> Within thy womb's well, deep and white,
> Whence streams a new-created age
> And golden light, and Golden Light![35]

Within Christianity, it is Mary, above all, who empowers Jesus, and who takes on the many titles and functions which we are here study-ing as qualities of the Goddess. However, the Orthodox teachings still address Mary:

> Hail, pure Lady, Mercy-Seat of the world;

> Hail, Ladder from earth which raised all to grace;
> Hail, Bridge which truly leads from death to life all those
> who praise thee.[1]

Isis was similarly accorded respect when twice a year her image was launched upon the waters in token of her patronage of the river Nile, whose rising provided the fertile soil for new growth. The voyage of Isis in her ship denotes the ability of the Empowerer to go forth at will and spread her merciful wisdom.[97]

Another mythic inheritor of Isis is Mary Magdalene, who, in the Gnostic scriptures reveals her ability to transmit wisdom. In this passage, she comforts the disciples in the upper room, after Jesus' resurrection from the dead: 'Peter said to Mary, "Sister, we know that the Saviour loved you more than the rest of women. Tell us the words of the Saviour which you remember – which you know [but] we do not nor have we heard them." Mary answered and said, "What is hidden from you, I will proclaim to you." And she began to speak to them . . .'[73] She proceeds to give the secret teachings. When Peter and Andrew question her sayings, Levi reproaches them, as she is the 'woman who knew the All', and her words are to be heeded. She is, in many ways, the earthly representative of Sophia, Lady Wisdom. *The Gospel of Philip* calls her 'the mother of angels'.[50]

The descent of Sophia from the fullness of the Pleroma (heaven) to create a new thing by herself, shows the delivering quality of the Empowerer. Both Sophia and the Shekinah involve themselves in coming close to creation, turning their backs on the transcendent roles which philosophers would save them for. If humankind are to be denied the glory of heaven, the fullness of bliss, then their part is to remain in exile with the rest of creation until the last blade of grass returns to the Pleroma before them. The continual presence of Sophia and the Shekinah among us, even in the heart of the most orthodox religious traditions, gives hope that the Goddess may truly be understood as Empowerer in our times.[63]

White Buffalo Woman appears among the Lakota tribe as Initiator and Empowerer. Her sacred gift is the pipe:

With this holy pipe . . . you will walk like a living prayer. With your feet resting upon the earth and the pipestem reaching into the sky, your body forms a living bridge between the Sacred Beneath and the Sacred Above. Wakan Tanka smiles upon us, because now we are as one: earth, sky, all living things, the two-legged, four-legged, the winged ones, the trees, the grasses. Together with the people, they are all related, one family. The pipe holds them all together.[100]

This great native American symbol of unity empowers the people to find their essential relationship with creation – an empowerment which is shared by the great European symbol, the Grail. The Grail is borne by many different bearers in different texts, yet the Grail Maiden is a true representative of the Empowerer. The Grail is the vessel empowerment which makes the wasteland fertile, which renders the despondent spirit joyous again. Its bearer has a companion, the Grail Messenger, who shows the way for the questing knights. The beautiful Grail Maiden and the ugly Grail Messenger between them bring about the restoration of creation, the first by her magnetic attraction, the second by her admonitory nagging. Together they show the dual face of the Empowerer.[58]

The Empowerer descends to the deepest foundations of our need. She applies remedies directly and addresses our needs directly. She gives rich gifts with great simplicity: food for the hungry, sovereignty in exchange for a kiss and healing by the application of like to like.

The treasures with which she empowers us have always been ours, but we have rejected them as too familiar, too ordinary. We have not used our greatest resources but the Empowerer has kept them for us, safe beyond hope and fear.

By her gifts we are at last empowered to use our own latent powers when we pass out of the Temple into the world. Her mysteries become the stuff of everyday life, for the living wisdom of the Empowerer becomes available to all as we exemplify it.

The Empowerer is, ultimately, the one who enables us to leave the formality of studying the Goddess by actively embodying her precepts in our own lives. We no longer visit the temple to be empowered, we *are* the temple and our hearts are her sanctuary.

We have come through the Temple of Light, through a bewildering multiplicity of forms and aspects of the Goddess. There remains one more aspect to experience. It is not named here for it is nameless, formless and empty, and only you can trace the shape, taste the flavour, sense the depth of this aspect. We can call it Space or Vastness, but we only grasp at words. It is the necessary void in which the jewel of the Temple of Light hangs. It is also at its heart, for whoever enters a holy place is immediately in relationship to the space demarked by the walls, ceiling and floor. It is into such a relationship that we must enter but we need not think of it as abstraction. In the words of Lady Yeshe Tsogyel who passed from human state to that of dakini and finally to that of Deliverer and Empowerer: 'wheresover is human emotion, there is sentient life; wheresoever is sentient life, there are the five elements; wheresoever are the five elements, there is space; and in so far as my compassion is co-extensive with space, it pervades all human emotion.[21]

This aspect is the pre-existent Light into whose glory the Shaper of All and all her aspects merge. She is the Space of Timeless Joy and Compassion whose music is the harmony of the spheres.

When we can be at ease dancing in space, all the forms and aspects of the Goddess will cease to be differentiated from each other, for we will have found the Goddess in truth. For, in the words of Sophia:

> I am the substance and the one who has no substance.
> Those who are without association with me are ignorant of me,
> and those who are in my substance are the ones who know me . . .
> And what you see outside of you,
> you see inside of you;
> it is visible and it is your garment . . .
> And you will find me there,
> and you will live
> and you will not die again.[73]

PART 3
DANCING IN SPACE

7. THE INNER TEMPLE

Whoever deeply searches out the truth
And will not be deceived by paths untrue,
Shall turn unto himself his inward gaze,
Shall bring his wandering thoughts in circle home
And teach his heart that what it seeks abroad
It holds in its own treasure chests within.

The Consolation of Philosophy
Boethius

In this part of the book, we will be exploring the interrelationships
of the ennead which we have just defined in detail. We have walked
through each of the circular chambers in the Temple of Light, but we
need to see just how the light of each of the Goddess' aspects colours
the others. Let us remind ourselves of the names of each aspect,
remembering that each one is derived from the Shaper of All:

1. **THE ENERGISER**
2. **THE MEASURER**
3. **THE PROTECTOR**
4. **THE INITIATOR**
5. **THE CHALLENGER**
6. **THE DELIVERER**

7. **THE WEAVER**
8. **THE PRESERVER**
9. **THE EMPOWERER**

Throughout Part 2, we drew from different world traditions in order to exemplify the nature and function of the nine aspects of the Shaper of All. We have even seen how, in just one Goddess such as Isis, for example, each of these nine aspects can be present and fully operative. There is never any question of the Goddess being limited to one form.

The next stage in the process of meeting the Goddess is to build your own inner Temple. You have already visited the Temple of Light, but it was rather like visiting a sacred site on . package tour. The speed at which you read will have dictated the length of your trip, but as the tour-guide, I may have hurried you through areas you would rather have lingered in, and probably lingered too long in places you thought of little interest or significance. This part of the book allows you to take your own trip at whatever speed you need.

The Temple you are going to build needs blueprints which only you can supply. The planning stages of your construction programme are crucial, so don't rush them. It may take very many months to get anywhere. If you rush your planning now, you are going to have to do some demolition later.

Let us look at a more simplified ground plan of the Temple. The central courtyard or chamber of this Temple is the Shaper of All – by whatever name you know her. The surrounding chambers all lead off from each other, only separated by veils, curtains or doors, as you wish. Each of the nine chambers leads into the central chamber.

Using a special note book or on a large sheet of paper, make your own plan of the Temple. Do not be worried that there seem to be no doors giving access to the Temple. This is an inner Temple which you will establish in your imagination. Desire follows thought, states the esoteric law, so as you wish, there you will be, in whatever chamber you desire.

Write down the aspects in order, with Shaper of All at the top, using your own knowledge and understanding of the Goddess to create your own array of aspects. These may derive from a specific mythology or spiritual tradition with which you are familiar, or you can combine mythologies using the most appropriate Goddesses to give you your own working chart of aspects. You may wish to constellate the aspects of one particular Goddess such as Kali or Isis, who have many clearly defined qualities or cultic devotions. If you have difficulty with any of the aspects, visualise the appropriate room in the Temple of Light, enter it and ask for help from that aspect.

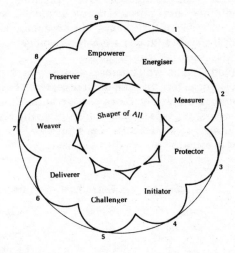

Fig.18 Temple of the Goddess – Inner Space and Sacred Mandala

Without consciously searching for a name or image, meditate on the meaning and significance of the aspect in question. Further questions to help provoke response and bring you practically into relationship with each aspect are given below.

As you are building a Temple, the first thing you should do is make a dedication. The dedication of a sacred site is always made as soon as the ground is levelled and made ready, but before any building work begins. You may want to set aside a special time of meditation on a suitable day, time or season. If you do not have an inkling about Goddess festivals, you might consult *Juno Covella: Perpetual Calendar of the Fellowship of Isis*, which lists an array of holy days associated with Goddesses from worldwide traditions.[24]

What dedication should you use? You can arrive at one in many different ways. You may wish to dedicate it to your own chosen Shaper of All, for example The Temple of Rhea. You could dedicate it to aspects or qualities to which you feel drawn, for example The Temple of Our Lady of Love and Wisdom. You may wish to dedicate it to a specific pantheon or mythology, for example The Temple of All Norse Goddesses. Or you may choose one Goddess and her many aspects such as The Nemeton (Sacred Grove) of the Ninefold Brighid.

Dedication makes your Temple operative on the inner planes. There are many people for whom a physical temple would be a great comfort but who have no space in their home. The advantage of your inner Temple is that it travels with you – wherever you are, it is also. All you have to do is construct it about you.

When meditating upon which named aspects you wish to install in your Temple, remember that you don't necessarily have to visualise them anthropomorphically. Since you are tuning to a frequency or energy of a specific aspect, don't be surprised if some express themselves through other symbolic forms such as pillars of colour or frequencies of sound.

CELTIC ASPECTS, COLOURS AND SYMBOLS

ASPECTS	GODDESSES	COLOURS	SYMBOLS
SHAPER OF ALL	Danu	Black	Milky Way
ENERGISER	Maeve	Blue	Bull
MEASURER	Macha	Grey	Cloak pin
PROTECTOR	Modron	Orange	Cloak
INITIATOR	Ceridwen	Yellow	Cauldron
CHALLENGER	Morrighan	Red	Spear
DELIVERER	Rhiannon	Violet	Key
WEAVER	Arianrhod	Indigo	Crystal tower
PRESERVER	Cessair	Green	Ship
EMPOWERER	Brighid	White	Flame

As my personal interest is in the Celtic tradition, I have given my own working plan as an example. If the Celtic tradition is also your own field of interest, you may disagree wildly with my list. Indeed, the list could be rearranged without too much difficulty into an alternative configuration drawing on different aspects of each Goddess. But you are free to use your own way of understanding. The important thing is that you arrive at a ninefold aspect which you can work with and if Freya is rubbing shoulders with Hera and Changing Woman, then don't worry. It is better not to mix traditions, but the criteria is – what works for you.

You are now ready to begin work on building and furnishing your Temple. The initial planning will take place in meditation (see page 106 for guidelines on meditation) when you visualise the ten chambers of the Temple. Skilful self-questioning will lead you through each of the aspects until you have at least one image of the Goddess represented in each chamber.

When you have each of the aspects, the next thing to do is to assign to your symbology a series of correspondences. I should stress that tables of correspondences can become very limiting and that they should be regarded only as the scaffolding upon which you manoeuvre in the early stages. When the Temple is built, the scaffolding comes down. Before you go on to more advanced work, you will need to dismantle this structure and consciously try to work without its supports. Indeed, careful work at this stage will result in greater clarity and integration later on.

In my example, I have listed only colours and symbols, but your list might include a whole variety of criteria, for example plants, gem stones, landscapes, kinds of weather, animals, music, an historical character who exemplifies the qualities of a specific aspect and so forth. Such a collection of criteria is made solely to fix the idea of the aspect in your understanding, although it can speedily become a mental junk shop unless you exercise great clarity. Nothing is fixed eternally, so expect your symbols to change as you change.

When you have a Goddess clearly established in each chamber of the Temple, meditate in each chamber on the symbolism of the different aspects. You might choose to start with: 'in what kind of weather does this aspect manifest?' You might decide that your chosen representation of the Energiser is best shown in a tornado or a gale force wind, for example, or the Preserver as gentle spring rain.

As you build up each new symbol or correspondence, so the Temple of Light will begin to come alive for you. You may find that the walls you so carefully erected between each chamber become concealed, that when you walk into another part of the Temple a whole landscape is forming, that the chamber of the Measurer has become an arena set under a calm, grey sky in a rocky landscape. Be imaginative and experience each aspect as fully as you know how, allowing the Temple of Light to become as wondrous and various as you like.

You may find that certain aspects are unclear to you or that you experience a very definite blockage whenever you sit down to meditate. Note these very carefully and determine to do more work on them, for without doubt you are recognising aspects of your own self to which you are resistant and which represent blindspots you consistently tend to avoid.

The following questions are suggestions only, but they may help uncover the hidden aspects which you have unconsciously overlooked:

SHAPER OF ALL: List words whose qualities suggest 'Goddess' to you. Where does your life feel most under pressure? Is this an urging to find greater fulfilment and possibility? What is the ground of your existence?

ENERGISER: What gets you going when you are in a rut? Are there any activities which give you energy? List energisers that you have known. What areas of your life need energising? Who do you resemble when you are energised?

MEASURER: Are there any defined limits to your activity? What kind of figures have defined the boundaries of your life? Which areas of your life need the Measurer most?

PROTECTOR: Describe your ideal Protector. List those who have protected you in your life. Where do you need protecting most and from what? How have you protected others?

INITIATOR: What do you imagine stands behind the door of the mysteries for you? Who do you imagine initiating you into these mysteries? What initiations have you passed up in your life? Which initiators have you known?

CHALLENGER: Do you see challenges as obstacles to overcome, or something to be confronted squarely? What challenges does life offer you? What recurrent patterns does your life keep throwing at you?

DELIVERER: From what do you need to be delivered? Where does your life suffer the worst blockages? List the deliverers you have known. When are you going to give up your sufferings and how?

WEAVER: Where in your life are your creative powers going? What masks do you wear in the world? If you had the power of a magician how would you use those powers? What areas of your life are most prone to self-deception?

PRESERVER: If the world ended tomorrow and a capsule was made available to you in which any thing, quality or concept could be saved, what would you put into it? What sustains your life physically, creatively and spiritually?

EMPOWERER: What treasures do you have? Which personal talents, abilities are you not making use of? How do you empower/disempower yourself?

These and other questions can be asked when you wish to explore your own response to particular aspects in meditation. With imaginative dedication, you will find that the Goddess in her many aspects will bring you to a better knowledge of yourself.

8. POWER OF THREE: POWER OF NINE

Building your Temple should take you a long time but you will become increasingly familiar with each shrine and begin to explore the relationships between each aspect indwelling there.

If you look at Fig.19 you will see that each spotlight circling the jewel's points also intersects four other circles of influence. The central aspect has especially strong relationships with the two circles furthest from it, for these bind together the chain of triadic links. In circle 1 you can see that the Protector of the Transforming Triad is in strong relationship to the Energiser, of the Dynamic Triad, and with the Challenger, of the Enfolding Triad. This gives us a new set of triadic relationships.

This diagram shows us all the possible permutations of interrelationships within the three triadic forms. Each of the alphabetical triads forms a new relationship of aspects which we would do well to explore in detail, for these give us new and exciting possibilities for working with the Goddess.

THE NINEFOLD TRIPLICITIES

	DYNAMIC	**ENFOLDING**	**TRANSFORMING**
A	*Energiser*	Preserver	Protector
B	*Initiator*	Measurer	Deliverer
C	*Weaver*	Challenger	Empowerer
	ENFOLDING	**TRANSFORMING**	**DYNAMIC**
D	*Measurer*	Empowerer	Initiator
E	*Challenger*	Protector	Weaver
F	*Preserver*	Deliverer	Energiser
	TRANSFORMING	**DYNAMIC**	**ENFOLDING**
G	*Protector*	Energiser	Challenger
H	*Deliverer*	Initiator	Preserver
I	*Empowerer*	Weaver	Measurer

The aspects in italics represent the focus of the triad, that is, the one which gives it its main character.

If we join each of the triplicities, we find that each forms an isosceles triangle, and that the full series of isosceles triangles form a nine-pointed star.

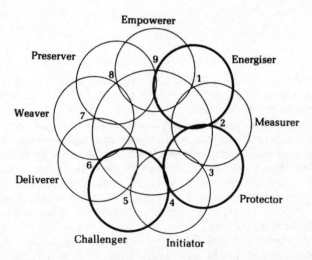

Fig. 19 The Triadic Links – showing the relationship of Energiser, Protector and Challenger

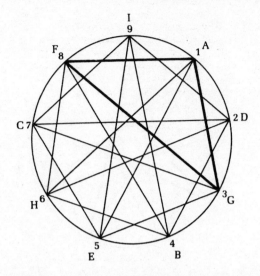

Fig. 20 The Ninefold Triplicities – showing the relationships of the Triad of Dynamic Guardianship: Energiser, Protector and Preserver

These new sets of triads can be called the Ninefold Triads:

A   The Triad of Dynamic Guardianship

B   The Triad of Dynamic Liberation

C   The Triad of Dynamic Potential

D   The Triad of Enfolding Power

E   The Triad of Enfolding Destiny

F   The Triad of Enfolding Health

G   The Triad of Transformative Wisdom

H   The Triad of Transformative Love

I   The Triad of Transformative Skill

Using your chosen aspects, take each triad in turn and meditate upon the qualities of each. A good method is to visualise yourself standing within a triangle formed of each of the relevant aspects. Taking the Triad of Enfolding Power as an example, imagine yourself facing the

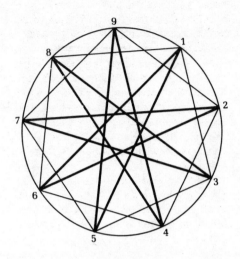

Fig. 21 Star of the Muses – this glyph can be drawn without lifting the pen from the page: starting at 9, draw to 2, to 4 etc. until the outside of the circle is joined at 9, then start the star drawing from 9 to 4 and so on.

Measurer, with the Empowerer on your left and the Initiator on your right. To strengthen the image, you may wish to visualise each of the aspects stretching out a length of cord to form the triangle in which you stand; the Measurer holding it out from either hand, and the Empowerer and the Initiator receiving it into their hands and passing it to each other, while you stand within its boundaries.

While you are meditating and learning about these relationships, you may well begin to wonder about the uses such permutations might have. In the early stages, it is hard to get a sense of perspective since your mind is grappling with unfamiliar concepts and associations. As you gain the ease and facility of devoted meditation, you will begin to realise that the Ninefold Triplicities can be used for the work of healing, both for yourself and for others. They also have wider uses.

If, for example, you wish to discover your true vocation in life you could visualise yourself standing in the Triad of Enfolding Destiny. To help an ailing friend you might visualise them within the Triad of Enfolding Health, receiving the healing of the three aspects you have chosen to represent the Preserver, the Deliverer and the Energiser. If you are in a stalemate situation where nothing is moving, try meditating within the Triad of Dynamic Liberation. When faced with a difficult individual with whom you feel irreconcilable differences, visualise both yourself and the other person within the Triad of Transformative Love.

In Fig. 21 we see that there is yet another way to look at the aspects of the Goddess. Throughout the world, the essential ninefold manifestation of the Mother is apparent. In Greece, there are the nine muses and their mother Mnemosyne; in Britain, the ninefold sisterhood of the cauldron and Ceridwen; in Arthurian legend, the ninefold sisterhood of Insula Pomorum – the Island of Apples or Avalon – where Morgen the Goddess and her sisters dwell.

In the Star of the Muses the nine aspects are each a point of the star and the centre space represents the Shaper of All. It is bounded by the Knot of the Philosophers, which runs about the circle. This glyph can be drawn without taking the pen off the page, as long as the connecting points are drawn first. Starting at any of the points, the nine straight lines about the circle are drawn first ending at the point where you began; then you can start drawing the interlocking star. Again, you can start at any point, mystically following the aspects of the Goddess in different ways.

Stop reading now and draw the Star of the Muses for yourself: trace over the circle and the points around it only, then number them and connect the lines starting at any point you choose, and using a ruler and compass if you need to. Now consider the route you have connected and meditate on the aspects in the order in which you have drawn them. When you have done that, shade in the pentacle or five-pointed star which stands prominently in the glyph, using a different, lighter colour to shade in the four remaining points.

From Fig. 21, we see that a pentacle can be formed of the Empowerer, the Measurer, the Initiator, the Challenger, and the Weaver. This pentad of powers gives you yet another way of working with the aspects in a relationship which is more complex and enriching than the triplicities or triads above. You will find that there are sets of mysteries locked within the many combinations, not all of which will be open to you. Other combinations will sometimes 'click' as you register them and it as though an independent holographic image deriving from all five aspects springs up in your understanding. Work round all the combinations until one pentad does this for you.

ASPECTUAL PENTADS

1. ENERGISER   PROTECTOR   CHALLENGER   DELIVERER   PRESERVER

2. MEASURER	INITIATOR	DELIVERER	WEAVER	EMPOWERER
3. PROTECTOR	CHALLENGER	WEAVER	PRESERVER	ENERGISER
4. INTIATOR	DELIVERER	PRESERVER	EMPOWERER	MEASURER
5. CHALLENGER	WEAVER	EMPOWERER	ENERGISER	PROTECTOR
6. DELIVERER	PRESERVER	ENERGISER	MEASURER	INITIATOR
7. WEAVER	EMPOWERER	MEASURER	PROTECTOR	CHALLENGER
8. PRESERVER	ENERGISER	PROTECTOR	INITIATOR	DELIVERER
9. EMPOWERER	MEASURER	INITIATOR	CHALLENGER	WEAVER

In each of the pentads, the other four aspects are also of great importance, for it is with their colouring that the pentads assume a distinct quality or mood. It is these shapings and patterns which will dictate the performance of certain mystery stories. Look at your chosen pentad and, using each aspect to hang your story upon, tell a spontaneous story to yourself. You will be amazed at how many stories you can tell. These will form the foundation of your own Goddess mysteries.

To give these tables and diagrams life, you will need to meditate diligently and find their practical applications, otherwise they will remain lists of theoretical permutations. The best language to translate them into reality is the language of ritual. By actually performing the symbolism, we come to understand it personally and immediately. If you are fortunate to work with a magical group you may have the opportunity to ritualise the nine aspects into nine roles, each officer representing one aspect. A tenth officer can take the part of the initiate and walk the route traced by the Star of the Muses and the Knot of the Philosophers. As he or she comes to each aspect, the two officers can ask questions of each other. Once you have a cycle of mystery stories, you will also be able to enact these ritually.

If you work alone, do not despair, you can still perform rituals on your own. To walk the Star of the Muses and the Knot of the Philosophers, you need only create a working area in which you place nine objects or pictures representing the aspects upon the ground in a circle. Sit in meditation in the middle to begin with and then pass to each point.

Whether working alone or with friends, choose to work on specific aspects, triads or pentads at each session, rather than attempting to work the whole Temple.

We come at last to the conclusion of the visualisation we began in Part 2 with the central star and its ninefold constellations. By its light, we have explored the Temple of Light and built our own inner Temple. As the Star of the Muses spirals off into space once more, be aware of the Goddess within you now, in all her aspects. She is your inner light, your maker, energiser, measurer, protector, initiator, challenger, deliverer, weaver, preserver and empowerer. You are her garment. It is now time for you to close this book and go out into the world and manifest her wherever you go.

> What else is the house of your mother
> and her room save the secret places
> of your inmost heart?
>
> St Ambrose

9. EARTHING AND ASPIRING

Her mind is full of excellent concentration,
Her manner, of playing in joy and delight,
Her diadem of the five deities sparklingly
Laughing with light – meditate on Her!

The Praise in Twenty-One Homages to Tara[96]

This section of practical exercises is included for all people who want to have a more than theoretical knowledge of the Goddess. Its title is indicative of the effects you can expect if you practise the exercises. The glamour of meditation and visualisation exercises is very potent and needs the counterbalance of practical application in one's own life. I have tried to ensure that all exercises follow this balanced pattern. All of them are applicable to either men or women.

A few words on performance: if you feel unwell, disorientated, confused, emotional or are taking drugs, leave these exercises alone until you have a measure of equilibrium. You need three basic senses in approaching this practice: common sense (your motherwit), a sense of proportion and a sense of humour. If you find yourself getting deadly serious, touchy, full of pride in your achievements as a priest/priestess of the Goddess, then take a break. Go and plant some seeds, wash out the pantry, clean the toilet or make some scones. More importantly, go and spend some time with people in the market-place, the park, or the launderette. Talk with them and ask yourself, 'how much of my spiritual practice is relevant to this person?' If you can't honestly think of anything, revise your practice speedily!

While earthing is important, we also need to aspire, to let our imaginations have free rein, to perceive possibilities and become prophetic or poetic. Many people have found that spending time with the Goddess gives them an access of freedom undreamt of; everything is suddenly possible, and even the dark days of financial gloom and emotional trauma are shot through with shafts of joy.

REANIMATING THE MYSTERIES OF THE GODDESS

We often wait for some mythical period in our future lives when we'll have the time and ability to begin spiritual practice but, be assured, this time will never come. So begin your own celebration of the Goddess exactly where you are and how you are *today*. Never mind what other people and groups are doing: determine your own practice and proceed in the light of her wisdom.

If you are the kind of person who likes to begin things formally, then sit down now and pick a day, next week or next month when you'll make time to start – *then stick to it*. But remember that today is always better than tomorrow, and every day is better than once a week.

Before reading on, begin now by making your dedication to the Goddess. It doesn't matter if you aren't sure who the Goddess is yet or where in your life she fits, so long as your heart yearns towards her. Wherever you are reading this, close your eyes and dedicate your efforts to understand her further. For example: *May my feet be set upon your paths*, or *Holy Mother* (Goddess' name/title) *I dedicate my study and spiritual practice to you. Help me to proceed by the light of your wisdom that I may know you better.*

One of the first prerequisites of reanimating the Mysteries of the Goddess in our time is the observation and practice of the simple everyday actions:

The simplest actions should be done with a full realization of their significance, giving them an opportunity to communicate their elemental meaning in our lives – pouring water from a jug, kneading bread, breaking an egg, observing the unconscious movements of those we love, working the earth, paring vegetables, singing a song . . . Through them God our Mother communicates with us through her body, within her own mysterious creation . . . We are physically signed with the earth symbols of the divine Generatrix.[15]

The mysteries of the Goddess must begin at home, for no amount of esoteric rites and practices will substitute for her presence in our lives. We cannot wait for special circumstances or conditions to arrive in our lives. The more constant your practice, the sooner you will see results. Habitual movements create their own circles of influence.

As soon as you can, set aside a day in which you can be totally in tune with these rhythms. This doesn't mean you can't do everyday tasks, just choose a day when you aren't moving house, interviewing for a new job or having a baby (at least until you are practised!). Get up earlier than you would normally, at dawn if possible, and greet the day.

Dedicate the day to the Goddess or one of her aspects. You could acknowledge the five elements, for example: *air* – yours is the precious and preserving air which enlivens me/us; *fire* – yours is the precious and preserving fire which warms me; *water* – yours is the precious and preserving water which purifies me; *earth* – yours is the precious and preserving earth which nourishes me; *spirit* – yours is the precious and pervading spirit within me. Everytime you come into contact with the elements, whether it is your first conscious breath of the day, switching on the gas fire, washing your hands, preparing and eating food or acknowledging the indwelling spirit which is in everything, your mundane actions can be a constant reminder of the Goddess.

Allow your every action, thought and desire to find its wise and compassionate balance. For the course of the day do not attempt to set up or insist upon your own structures but 'go with the flow'. Mark the four points of the day in acknowledgement of the Goddess: dawn or rising, midday, twilight and midnight or sleeping.

MEDITATING AND VISUALISING

To construct your inner temple, you are going to become a skilled meditator and visualiser. If this statement alarms you, be assured that you already possess the capabilities of becoming both. Meditation is simply a condition in which you set aside the cares of the day, make a quietness within you and enter that waiting stillness. During meditation we may become aware of deeper realisations concerning our lives or of a specific subject of contemplation; in the stillness we may visualise many things.

There are many ways of learning a subject but all courses of instruction include both theory and practice. Meditation takes us into another level of training, where we must interact with our subject with no intervening teacher, book or material. Meditation gives us the 'proving stage' of the learning process where the materials are set ready and the method is practically used. It is also where the subtle communion between ourselves and the subject becomes critically important so that we may be able to distinguish the workman from the work of art – for meditation is an art.

To begin meditating, decide on a place and time which must be consistent, quiet and special to you. It may be no more than a chair in your bedroom or kitchen at a time of day when you are going to be undisturbed – a space you can call your own. If you have a shrine you can meditate in front of it, but otherwise setting up a framed picture or visual aid in front of you as a focus will suffice. This is not strictly necessary but when you begin meditating it is sometimes a help.

In meditation we eliminate all causes of physical, mental and spiritual stress. All meditation requires an upright, supported posture, which is why Eastern meditators adopt the lotus position, but this is not essential. The normal meditation posture for the West is to be seated upright on a hard chair with a back, and possibly a footstool or cushion to raise the knees level with your hips. Your hands can lie along your thighs or be clasped loosely in your lap.

Quieting our minds and clearing spiritual blockages is a lot harder than relaxing our bodies. Always spend about five minutes before your main meditation session in basic preparation. Sit in your meditation space and concentrate on establishing a comfortable, supported posture. Next observe your breath, which is the most indicative sign of our inner condition. When we are busy we often forget to breathe evenly, sometimes even holding our breath until an action is performed. As you settle into position, let your breathing purposely become very deep and slow for a few inhalations, and then let it find its natural rhythm.

If you are unused to rhythmic breathing or unsure about how to do this, as an experiment you can lie down on your bed and lay a hand on your diaphragm. As you lie at rest, you will feel your hand rising and falling. That is the kind of breathing that is required. (However, do not attempt to do any concentrated meditation lying down as you will fall asleep!)

Finding initial stillness may require a good deal of practice. Meditation time should not be spent thinking of your bad day at work or compiling your shopping list, although intrusive thoughts do come to us all. Make a verbal affirmation of your intention, for example:

> I am entering the stillness before creation,
> I am entering the ground of the Goddess.
> May my body be still,
> May my mind be peaceful,
> May my heart be ready.
> May all that I realise today benefit all creation.

Or you can make up your own affirmation. Take a few minutes to breathe into your meditation.

Now, you are ready to begin meditating in truth. In this book, the main forms of meditation described are visual, although there are many other kinds of meditation – both with and without form. Visualisation is a very Western form of realising and fixing your meditation. Most people are skilled visualisers in everyday life; we can remember where and on which shelf that book we need is kept, where certain shops are in relation to each other, how to get from A to B. For all these actions we visualise an existing structure: our bookshelf, our street or a road map.

In the construction of your inner temple, you are really dancing in space to begin with, for all that you possess is the ground plan and a few basic descriptions of the Goddess' aspects. This basic travel information must be supplemented by first hand experience for, unlike earthly locations and sites which are unchanging regardless of the visitors, your visualisation will provide intimately personal landscapes and images.

First visualise where you need to be and state your intention once more, for example:

> Swiftly, surely, without fear,
> I seek the shrine of the Deliverer.
> From this place to that place,
> From my time to her time,
> Under the protection of the Shaper of All.

Strive to be there, do not see yourself as on a television. If your visualisation is unclear, ask questions of yourself such as: is it day or night when you step into the shrine of the Deliverer? How is it furnished? What symbols or objects do you see? What image forms the focal point?

Learn to trust the first thing you see, even if the image seems inappropriate at first. You can ask questions of what or whoever you meet in your visualisation. If you see a basket of fruit in the shrine of the Deliverer ask the image or the basket itself 'what is the significance of this image?'

Gradually you will build up confidence and become an experienced traveller within. Always remember to leave the scene and close the session properly. In conclusion you can say: 'I have walked in the Temple of Light, in the shrine of the Deliverer. From her place to my place, from her time to my time, under the protection of the Goddess'. Or if you have had a general meditation on another topic say:

> I return from the stillness before creation,
> I return from ground of the Goddess.
> May my body be wakeful,
> May my mind be alert,
> May my heart be open,
> May all I have realised benefit all creation.

Always record in a special note book your realisations and experiences from meditations, as like dreams, they will fade rapidly.

YOUR INNER GUIDE

There are many methods of enabling us to find an inner or spiritual guide to help us progress.[66,91] It is possible that you may want to discover one for the first time or to contact a guide who is best suited to your growing understanding of the Goddess. How do you go about this?

Not far from the Temple of Light is a cave wherein your inner guide lives. He or she is in the service of the Goddess and the guide's task is to act as your helper and instructor. Sit in meditation and visualise a path before you. Follow it, for it leads to the cave of your guide. In the entrance of the cave a fire is burning. As you sit down beside it your guide will emerge from the cave and sit opposite you. You may see a man or a woman, for the guide can be a priest or priestess of the Temple of Light whose task is to help travellers who seek the Goddess. Visualise your guide very clearly and ask by what name they should be known. Your guide is not a deity but an excarnate human being of whom you may ask many questions. It may take more than one session to see and communicate with your guide, so persevere.

Your guide will answer questions relevant to your spiritual unfolding which may involve a closer look at your present life style or a change of direction for you. Always weigh what your guide says for truth, personal relevance and effectiveness, especially if you are fearful of 'pushing' the advice by self-suggestion. You should feel easy with your guide, not intimidated or overawed.

Your guide will help you begin the establishment of your inner temple. Ask him or her to lead you there. At the back of the cave is an underground tunnel which leads to the foundations of the temple. (Below the temple itself, you may later establish a chamber wherein you can incubate dreams and have them interpreted by your guide.) At any point of difficulty or decision during the building process, your guide will assist you. Ask skilful questions and listen well.

MEETING THE GODDESS

We each meet the Goddess on our own ground and in our own ways. She is not a remote figure, although if you have not yet made conscious contact with her, you may think she is. The old religious models in which we were raised give us an awe of approaching the divine and very possibly also a kind of high-flown 'god-speak' in which to communicate. Let us leave these models by the roadside, for they will not serve us here.

Let us meet the Goddess first as Mother, and gain the confidence and intimacy of a child in relating to her. It is helpful but not essential to perform this exercise with another person to act as 'midwife'. If you are doing this alone, your inner guide will perform this function for you. Either record this script or get your partner to read it out aloud to you, leaving suitable pauses for realisation.

The process of birth which is experienced in this visualisation may be a traumatic subject of meditation for some readers, but at no point should any obstetric difficulties arising from the reader's own birth be replayed in this scenario. This exercise has nothing whatever to do with the New Age practice of Rebirthing, nor should it be conflated with any of its techniques.

Go back to the time before you were born or conceived. You are in primordial space, beyond the dimensions of time and place with which you are familiar. Everything exists potentially in primordial space. You are a soul without a form to manifest within, waiting tranquilly for the call to incarnate. From deep within primordial space, feel an urgent and clear calling which is intended for you and you only. Go directly to the source of that calling. As you pass instantly to that source you are aware of other potentialities swirling down about it, rather as bees gravitate to the hive. You may be aware of different energies, colours or patterns which swirl and coalesce as you reach your goal.

The call is being emitted from a deep vessel within primordial space. It calls all the potential parts of your incarnate self within itself. For the first time, you, as pure spirit, begin to feel the formative powers of the four elements gathering about you. Your physical shape is being formed of the earth and water of matter, it is veined with the fire of blood and the inspiration of air. You are now a living, incarnate spirit yet to be born. Within the vessel of the womb, you are aware of the rushing of liquid, the slow steady rhythm of a heart. The only sense you can exercise in the womb is that of instinct and your instinct tells you that you are protected and guarded from all harm, and so you are comfortable in your growing state.

You are growing all the time, becoming more and more mature. Your limbs and organs are now fully formed and it is time to completely enter the dimension of four elements, wherein your incarnate spirit will commence its next cycle. You are ready to be born. The sides of the vessel now urge and impel you outwards. For you, the process of birth is as logical and smooth as your incarnation. Your life task awaits you as you emerge into light.

(Your 'midwife' partner should be very sensitive to this part of the exercise, if necessary assisting and comforting you.)

Your inner guide is there to help you to be born, to bathe and clothe you. S/he then hands you – a newborn human being – to the mother. Your eyes are open and you see your mother for the first time – it is the Goddess herself from whose womb you have been born. She sets you to her breast and gives you nourishment. The bonds between you are immediate and familiar. Your heart is glad. At the breast of the Goddess you receive not only physical but spiritual sustenance. Feel her arms about you and hear her speak your secret name.

Awaken now, child of the Goddess, and return to your own time and place as an adult human being.

You may wish to write your own visualisations wherein you meet the Goddess at various crucial points of your own life cycle: first experience of education, rites of passage at adolescence, beginning of the menarche, first sexual encounter or marriage . . . Whatever your actual experience in this life, this exercise can help you encounter the Goddess in a transformative scenario which may clear problems arising from a lack of initiatory awareness.

You can similarly write a visualisation for your own death. The West has little or no effective methods of preparing for death, so that periodic meditation upon returning to the Shaper of All can be very helpful. When death does come, and it comes for every created thing, it is better to be thus prepared and fully aware that it is but one stage in the cycles of becoming.

TRANSFERENCE OF LIGHT

Some of the following exercise call for the Transference of Light. This is performed when you are within the Temple of Light or are visualising the Goddess or one of her aspects. It should be utilised only when you have fully conceptualised and visualised the Goddess. The Transference of Light is intended to align your purpose with that of the Goddess or her aspect.

Visualise the Goddess clearly. Next visualise a clear ray of light beaming from her heart to yours. As you experience this, feel the warmth and radiance of her compassion enter and remain with you. *The light-transference should not be attempted until a vividly clear visualisation immediately precedes it*. This is important because any lack of clarity, whether of visualisation or of intention, may cause personality problems. The Transference of Light is a direct empowering by the Goddess – you are enabled to share her compassionate view of the world. This empowering should enhance her presence *through* you as her agent, it is not about behaving in a high-handed way. Cultivate a sense of gratitude in her merciful compassion as you perform this exercise and you will guard against the human tendency towards pride.

SHRINE-MAKING

There are few people today who have space for a physical temple of their own but even in the most crowded home there is room for a shrine on a shelf or dresser. Those who share a home with family or friends who are unsympathetic to their spiritual practice will not offend anyone by putting a folding picture frame and a vase of flowers in their room.

According to your personal tastes, your mythological and aspectual devotion, create a sacred space for your shrine. Make sure it is clean and sweet smelling. You can first purify the area by blessing it with the four elements: a sprinkling of earth and water, a candle and an incense stick for fire and air. Dress your shrine with intention, leaving the installation of the central picture, image or statue until last. You may wish to invite friends to help you consecrate your shrine and see it become operational.

Shrine making is a natural activity with very few rules. The most important of these is: be sure you have time to care for your shrine properly. By setting one up you are welcoming the power of the Goddess into your home. If you neglect it or have too many shrines about your home, you may be unable to tend them responsibly. Your shrine will begin to resemble your own spiritual state – cluttered, dusty, untended and lifeless.

If you cannot have a perpetual light burning on your shrine, try and ensure that you spend at least a few moments there daily when the candle is lit. If you make a habit of this you will ensure that your working relationship with the Goddess remains lively.

DIGGING UP BURIED TREASURE

There is an esoteric law which states: 'Thought follows desire'. This is another way of saying: 'Where your heart is, there your treasure is also'.

The Goddess in all her aspects is typified by compassionate wisdom in action. She answers our need as directly as bread assuages hunger, as love-making satisfies sexual need. Life is about an exchange of energy, but we seldom use the whole of ourselves and often reserve our best energies for some legendary time when we'll be able to use them to good effect. If this is the case, it is not just the Old Woman Under the Hill who has been devalued, it is also our own inner treasures which have been set aside 'for a special occasion'. Unlock your treasures now and propose ways of using them.

The Goddess gives us access to our creative and imaginative levels, which are so often denied any use in daily life because our society sets a low value on these commodities – at least in people whose daily work is considered 'non-creative'. Of course, all work like all play, has to be creative to some degree or our lives would corrode. Because we seldom allow ourselves space to enjoy our treasures, they begin to lose their savour and our lives become subsequently impoverished. So let's discover what our hidden treasures are.

Visualise the shrine of the Empowerer as clearly as you can or set up a physical altar to her. Bring offerings of respect: flowers, fruits of the earth or of your creative skills. Now meditate on the Empowerer as the giver and guardian of gifts. See her with her emblems and symbols and make the Transference of Light (see page 112).

Let her light permeate your body, bringing illumination to the dark places within you. The Empowerer asks you: 'What are your treasures?' Briefly review your own talents, abilities, aptitudes and skills.

The Goddess asks: 'How do you use them?' Answer honestly, reviewing the amount of energy you really put into practising these treasures. Make an offering of them now, visualising them symbolically and committing them to the service of the Goddess. The Empowerer accepts them with her own hands, absorbing them into herself.

The Empowerer now asks you: 'What are your deepest needs?' Look into the areas of your life where you feel least confident, most fearful, most unhappy. If you cannot get to the root of your need, the Empowerer asks: 'What worries you most now?' Answering this will help trace your deepest needs, which we often suppress in case we ever have to face them properly, even on a mental level. If admitting these needs causes pain, remember that you have made the Transference of Light and are in the full protection of the Goddess – she will support you.

Now offer these needs to the Goddess as sincerely as you can, visualising them symbolically just as you offered her your treasures, for these are also you. As you do so the Empowerer accepts them with her own hands, absorbing them into herself. But this time she transforms them. Visualise a ray of sparkling red light streaming from her heart into yours: this light also gives warmth and strength to meet your needs. Allow it to permeate your body and gives thanks. You may also be aware of the Empowerer holding something in her hands which she gives to you. This will be symbolic of your hidden treasure, an unknown resource which will help you to be more effective in your life. If the significance of this object or symbol is unclear to you, ask the Empowerer to tell you about it.

HEALING THE EARTH

Acknowledging that we are part of the earth is very important, for it is the Goddess' creation. We live in an age which is reaping the results of generations of human wilfulness. There are many New Age and pagan associations which have established themselves as earth guardians, but this is really the task of everyone living on the planet. Apart from a more responsible ecological attitude, we can also do a great deal towards the healing and preserving of the planet by esoteric means. Indeed, without inner intention, even corporate political acts come to nothing.

For this exercise, enter your fully operative Temple of Light. You will be working in the central shrine of the Shaper of All. Visualise a great black mirror there set into the ground. See, lying in the depths of the mirror as though in a deep pool, the earth itself. Dedicate the planet to the Shaper of All under the name you use, and ask her to bless and preserve it. Now, working with each aspect of the nine surrounding shrines, see in the mirror a star whose light beams down upon the earth and enhances the quality of that aspect. For example, with the Energiser: see the power of the Energiser beaming down upon the earth, sweeping away sloth and outworn ideas which are obstructing the perfect health of the planet and its life forms.

Work through a single aspect in each session, first dedicating the earth to the Shaper of All, and spend at least ten minutes visualising the effect of each aspect upon the planet.

BLESSING AND ROOTING UP

We each possess the indwelling spirit of an incarnate human being, in intimate and familial relationship to the Goddess, whom we may see as the source of spirituality. This places us each in a unique position to bestow blessings wherever we go. When a thing or action is blessed it partakes of her spirit. We can increase our capacity for joy and wisdom by blessing. Nearly everywhere else, save in the spiritual desert of the civilised Western world, people bestow or ask blessings upon every action they perform. Jews, for example, ask blessings upon every physical human function, such as drinking, eating, smelling and so on. Catholics ask priests to bless new houses, children and rosaries.

We can bring blessings to our own everyday lives and those about us in very simple ways. In the name of the Goddess we can bless domestic actions, the tools of our work, people with whom we come into contact, as well as asking blessings upon our own plans and those of others.

We each possess the power to bless and to root things up. Blessings are something we all like the sound of, but rooting up may sound a bit like cursing. As we have noticed throughout this book, the Goddess is concerned with creation but she is also the mistress of destruction. She includes the catabolic ability to break down structures as well as to build them. If there was no law of destruction on earth, there would be no decay and reassimilation of matter. Just imagine a world where no dead thing decayed, where rubbish didn't burn, where nothing made could be destroyed. The Goddess mercifully grants death and decay to all created things.

This is why we speak here of rooting up rather than cursing. Cursing is a negative action carrying its own karmic debt which, like thoughtless words or unspoken destructive thoughts directed against another, have no part in the Goddess' framework. Rooting up is about the controlled eradication of whatever is outgrown or decaying within our world or psyche.

Rooting up should begin and end with ourselves. For while we may freely give blessings to all and any, rooting up needs a larger perspective than humanity can achieve. The daily self-clarification whereby we check up on our intentions, actions and bad habits should give us ample opportunities to request this function. Whatever is outgrown within other people is not your concern; give blessing to such people and ask the Goddess to manage the work of rooting up if this is required. Similarly, if you are aware of something or somebody blocking the wise working of the world and the effective living of its created forms, request that the Goddess sees to it in her own way and time. Thus, the eradication of whatever is not beneficial or outworn remains the full responsibility of the Goddess, not ourselves. Whether we request blessing or rooting up, let it be with no self-interest but with total compassion.

RITUAL COMMUNION

Ritual communion with the Goddess is likely to sound like a parody of the Christian mysteries to you unless you are aware of the fact that nearly every agricultural society of prehistory presented the first fruits of the earth to the Goddess, baking cakes and brewing beer in her honour as offerings. This exercise involves your active creation of the ritual elements, for you are going to make cakes and an approximation of the Eleusinian mystery drink.

To make the drink, go to a health shop and buy a small bag of barley grains, a lemon and some (culinary, not perfumed) mint. Steep about two good handfuls of the barley in a half pint of boiling water. Add the juice of the lemon and a pinch of mint and leave overnight in a covered bowl. In the morning, strain it through a sieve or muslin net. It is now ready for use.

To make the cakes, you need a flour with no raising agent in it (preferably organic flour, but any kind will do, and use the sacred grain of your region if you can: corn, maize, rice, wheat), salt, butter, milk, a little spice (cinnamon, mixed spice or ginger), a baking tray, a mixing spoon and bowl. Measure out about five handfuls of flour (1½ cups) in the bowl and add the spice. (If you need it add a little sugar or honey for sweetness.) Rub about 2–3 oz of cold butter (2–3 heaped dessert spoonfuls) into the flour. Add the milk only if necessary: the mixture should be tacky and stick to the fingers but not feel wet. Either roll out thinly or shape your cakes by hand into whatever shape you want, for example, a crescent moon, or a star. Bake on a greased tray at gas mark 5 (375⁰F or 150⁰C) for about ten to fifteen minutes, or until golden. Set to cool.

You now have your cakes and sacred drink: now put them in suitable containers. If you've nothing special use your own daily crockery, but it's nicer to have special vessels and plates, especially if you can buy some quick-dry clay and fire it in your oven.

You will probably want to perform your communion at special times, such as full moons, fire-festivals or solstices, but use your own calendar. Devise a short, simple ritual, dedicating the cakes and drink you have made in the Goddess' name. Bless them and partake of them in silence, acknowledging the Goddess. Share them with friends. If anything is left over, give it to the elements, but always reserve a libation of drink and a cake for the Mother herself.

THE CYCLIC YEAR

Nowadays we tend to live by clocks rather than by the natural unfolding cycles of the agricultural and seasonal year. But all of life takes place in the Mother's good time. We know that to rush something is often to spoil it, but we keep trying to fit in more and more things on our agenda only to find that we are too stale to perform any of them. People, like plants, follow the natural cycle of seeding, nurturing, growing, resting, decay and reseeding.

Finding the cyclic rhythms of our existence is another important factor in the Mysteries of the Goddess. Discover the rhythm of the day, divided into dawn, noon, twilight and midnight; of the month, marked by the changing phases of the moon in its waxing, full, waning and dark aspects; of the year in its seasons of spring, summer, autumn and winter; and of our own life cycle – childhood, adolescence, maturity and old age. Make your own calendar from a consideration of these rhythms and find new patterns of living within it.

Many people now observe the cyclical pattern of the Celtic fire festivals, the solstices and equinoxes, as well as the moon's phases for their celebration of the Goddess. Working with the ninefold aspects with the Shaper of All as the co-ordinating aspect of the Goddess, you may wish to celebrate these in a meaningful way throughout the seasons. You may wish to honour the major triads on the main phases of the moon: the Transforming Triad on the new moon, the Dynamic Triad on the waning moon, the Enfolding Triad at the full moon, the Shaper of All herself as the potential of the dark phase of the moon. You may wish to write a ritual to be performed in a seasonal cycle, in which the fivefold aspects (see page 101) are the basis for your own mystery sequence. This is a matter of personal preference and aptitude, as well as of seasonal observation. Be inventive in your celebrations of the Goddess and find her energy in every part of your life.

GODDESS ROSARY

String a series of beads, crystals or other appropriate objects on a chain or length of knotted cord. Many craft shops sell equipment to make such things but all you will basically need is a length of strong nylon thread and some beads. You can make your Goddess rosary in two different ways, using single beads for each of the nine aspects and a special one for the Shaper of All herself, or else a series or cluster of beads for each aspect.

Create a series of prayers, mantras or invocations to go with each bead. As an example, for the Shaper of All: 'Mother, you have made and shaped me, honour and serenity are yours. I am your garment; you the indwelling spirit. Work through me in everything I do, that all may know you. For each aspect (insert your own preferred name as well as or instead of the suggested title as you wish): Lady Energiser, quicken me. Sister Measurer, clear my path. Protecting Mistress, guard me safely. Initiating Mother, take my hand. Cailleach, Challenger, transform me. Saving Lady, be my help. Weaver of the Web, make my pattern bright. Mother and Preserver, heal me. Empowering Daughter, make me wise'. These are examples only showing the range of titles you might use. Of course you need not only ask things for yourself but also for others, or else frame you words as venerations or statements of that power.

You can say your rosary when you are alone at any time. Rather than going round the whole chain, you can pray with a particular triad of mysteries each day: the Transforming Mysteries on Tuesdays and Fridays, the Dynamic Mysteries on Wednesdays and Saturdays, the Enfolding Mysteries on Thursdays and Sundays, and on Monday pray with the whole chain, with special emphasis on the Shaper of All. Alternatively, allot your rosary to days most appropriate to your manner of working.

BEYOND THE ELEMENTS OF THE GODDESS

The integration of your practice and understanding is going to take some time. For advanced work, you will probably discard the structure of the Temple which you built or will eventually be able to move beyond its confines into other areas. The myth of progress is a hard one to crack, but you should be aware that this work with the Goddess is one of forgetting and remembering. While you will always be able to find the main wavebands, you may have to twiddle the switches to find other stations which will seem to slew about on the airwaves in a disconcerting manner. This happens because the Goddess brings about the assimilation and merging of different parts of yourself, the learning process is thus dependent upon your individual make up and its permutations are impossible to predict.

Continual practice is the only known method of staying in touch with anything. Even virtuoso instrumentalists know that while practice improves technique, it never makes truly 'perfect', and that a day's practice lost means a less efficient technique.

Going beyond the elements of the Goddess is your adventure which no one can organise in advance, let alone yourself. There will be moments, infrequent at first, but increasing in intensity, when you will feel that the divisions between you and the Goddess are pretty thin, that you are of one mind and heart. In speaking of these mystical fields of experience, let us be clear and frank with ourselves, for the same semantic problems occur here as they do in attempting to describe the Goddess in symbolic language. We live in a dualistic world which divides experience from the experiencer. In the mystical field, there are no such divisions, only a sense of unity, union or communion. It is not an experience which can be achieved by intellectual effort or spiritual merit, rather it is as though *we* were the spinning arm of the compass and the *Goddess* was true north. We veer over this point of harmonious contact times without number until our instinct brings us into alignment and we consciously recognise it. But even this image fails because in this state of alignment, we *become* both the compass and true north itself. We are the quest and its goal at once.

When you understand the previous paragraph from your own personal experience rather than intellectual theory, you are ready to 'assume the Goddess'. This advanced method of working is rarely taught in the West, but it was once part of the ancient mystery school teachings where it was applied to all deities. It is still the experience of the shamans and shamankas of all native traditions.

Please do not attempt the following practice if you have a history of psychological disorder such as schizophrenia, or if you are using any consciousness changing drugs (whether prescribed or not), or if you are in a disoriented or emotional condition. You will receive no benefits but only further confusion. If you are in any doubts about your fitness to perform the Assumption of the Goddess, either ask your inner guide or go into the shrine of the Challenger and ask her. She will forthrightly test your fitness by appropriate questions or tests. Trust her judgement.

To assume a deity we must first of all be in a state of purity – this means the purification of body, mind and spirit. Impurity blocks alignment and accentuates human imbalances. This practice is performed after fasting, after a ritual bath and with clean garments. It is preceded by a period of self-clarification and meditation. Next comes the generation of the image of the chosen aspect of the Goddess. For this, you simply follow your normal visualisation procedure, making fullest use of the symbolism you have associated with the chosen aspect. With invocations and prayers which you have made, invite the chosen aspect to unite with you.

Make the usual Transference of Light (see page 112) but this time you will see the light penetrating to your innermost being and purifying all that obscures your understanding – every ignorance, desire and hatred will be purified. Visualise yourself as the chosen aspect and receive her empowering energy. At this point, there are no divisions between you and the subject of your meditation. Abiding in this state, be filled with the full realisation of yourself as the Goddess.

When you first perform the Assumption of the Goddess, conclude your meditation by slowing absorbing the image into your heart and re-establish consciousness immediately. This experience is beyond worship or veneration, it is pure being and identification. You will understand from the nature of this advanced practice why purification is so important and why it is not lightly performed. It is especially important to acknowledge your own imbalances beforehand and to ask the Goddess to help you to balance them through every action in your daily life.

Once you have performed this practice, you will be taught its further uses by the Goddess herself. This initiation passes beyond the confines of either this book or your self-built Temple. When you have experienced all aspects of the Goddess in this manner, you may indeed call yourself her priest or priestess.

May the Awakener, the Transformer and Enfolder bless you and bring you into the real presence of the Shaper of All!

You have discovered the changing faces of the random Goddess. To others she still veils herself, but to you she has revealed herself to the full.

Boethius

GLOSSARY OF GODDESSES

The following is a list of Goddess names used in this book. Rather than take up valuable space repeating details about each Goddess I have preferred to index them separately here, giving a brief description of their main functions or qualities, and the page numbers where they are referred to. Of course, these Goddesses have far more aspects and functions than are listed here.

Aditi (Hindu) the cow of cosmic space 40

Amaterasu (Japanese) sun 79

Ambika (Hindu) 'Little Mother', aspect of **Kali** 55

Ananke (Greek) necessity 49

Angerboda (Norse) creator 50–51

Anu (Celtic) primal ancestress 41

Aphrodite (Greek) love 38, 45

Ariadne (Minoan) star, leader through the maze 77

Arianrhod (British) initiator 62, 94

Artemis (Greek) huntress 56–7

Astarte (Babylonian) love and war 45

Athene (Greek) war, patron of Athens 51, 56, 62

Atropos (Greek) measurer of the life thread, one of the **Moirae** 49

Bagala (Hindu) one of the **Dasa-Mahavidyas**, protector 31

Baubo (Greek) energiser 45

Beltia (Babylonian) 'the Lady', the heavens 53

Bhairavi (Hindu) one of the **Dasa-Mahavidyas**, weaver 31

Bhunaneshvari (Hindu) one of the **Dasa-Mahavidyas**, preserver, Shaper of All 31

Black Virgin (Christian) dark and healing aspect of **Mary** 30

Bona Dea (Roman) 'the Good Goddess', patron of women's rites 14

Brighid (Irish) healing, smithcraft, poetry 57, 81–3, 94

Cailleach (Celtic) dark aspect 66

Ceres (Roman) agriculture 80

Ceridwen (British) initiator 59–60, 74–5, 100

Cessair (Irish) primal ancestress 94

Changing Woman (Native American) transformer, *see* **Estanalehi** 94

Chinnamasta (Hindu) one of the **Dasa-Mahavidyas**, *also* **Varjayogini**, initiator 31, 65

Cipactli (Mexican) creator 41

Circe (Greek) shapeshifter and weaver 72, 74

Clotho (Greek) Spinner of the thread, one of the **Moirae** 49

Corn Maidens (Native American) givers of grain and wisdom 79

Cybele (Thracian) great mother 5, 14, 47, 59

Daena (Persian) Challenger on the bridge of the Afterlife 66

Dakini (Tibetan) 'sky-dancer', meditational female deity 43–5, 70, 87

Danu (Irish) primal ancestress 94

Dasa-Mahavidyas (Hindu) the ten wisdom aspects of **Kali** 31

Demeter (Greek) initiator 46, 60, 68–9, 73, 80

Devi (Hindu) Hindu for 'Goddess' 46

Dhatisvari (Hindu) **dakini** of 'mirror-like wisdom', ruler of east and water 43

Dhumavati (Hindu) one of the **Dasa-Mahavidyas**, challenger 32

Diké (Greek) justice 51

121

BIBLIOGRAPHY

GENERAL

1.   *The Akathist Hymn & Little Compline*, Faith Press, n.d.
2.   Allione, Tsultrim, *Women of Wisdom*, Routledge & Kegan Paul, 1984.
3.   Argüelles, Miriam & José, *The Feminine, Spacious As the Sky*, Shambhala, 1977.
4.   Auden, W. H. & Taylor, Paul B. *Norse Poems*, Faber, 1981.
5.   Bakhtiar, Laleh, *Sufi Expressions of the Mystic Quest*, Thames & Hudson, 1976.
6.   Begg, Ean, *The Cult of the Black Virgin*, Arkana, 1985.
7.   Berger, Pamela, *The Goddess Obscured*, Beacon Press, 1985.
8.   Beyer, Stephan, *The Cult of Tara*, University of California Press, 1971.
9.   Bierhorst, John, ed. *The Red Swan: Myths & Tales of the American Indians*, Farrar, Straus & Giroux, 1976.
10. Blacker, Carmen, *The Catalpa Bow: a Study of Shamanistic Practices in Japan*, Allen & Unwin, 1975.
11. Blofield, John, *Compassion Yoga: the Mystical Cult of Kwan Yin*, Allen & Unwin, 1977.
12. Boethius, *The Consolation of Philosophy*, trans. V. E. Watts, Penguin, 1969.
13. Carmichael, Alexander, *Carmina Gadelica*, Scottish Academic Press, 1972.
14. Clark, Ella E. *Indian Legends of Canada*, McClelland & Steward Ltd., 1960.
15. Craighead, Meinrad, 'Immanent Mother' in *The Feminist Mystic*, ed. Mary E. Giles, Crossroad, New York.
16. Craighead, Meinrad, *The Mother's Songs: Images of God the Mother*, Paulist Press, 1986.
17. Cross, T. P. & Slover, C. H. *Ancient Irish Tales*, Figgis, 1936.
18. Crossley–Holland, Kevin, *The Norse Myths*, André Deutch, 1980.
19. Crowley, Vivianne, *Wicca: the Old Religion in the New Age*, Aquarian Press, 1989.
20. Dalai Lama, The; Tsong-Ka-Pa & Hopkins, Jeffrey, *Deity Yoga*, Snow Lion Publications, 1987.
21. Dowman, Keith, *Sky Dancer: the Secret Life and Songs of the Lady Yeshe Tsogyel*, Routlege & Kegan Paul, 1984.
22. Durdin–Robertson, Lawrence, *The Goddesses of Chaldea, Syria and Egypt*, Cesara Publications, 1973.
23. Durdin–Robertson, Lawrence, *The Goddesses of India, Tibet, China and Japan*, Cesara Publications, 1974.

24. Durdin–Robertson, Lawrence, *Juno Covella: Perpetual Calendar of the Fellowship of Isis*, Cesara Publications, 1982.
25. Eisler, Riane, *The Chalice and the Blade*, Harper and Row, 1988.
26. Evola, Julius, *The Metaphysics of Sex*, East–West Publications, 1983.
27. Feinstein, David & Krippner, Stanley, *Personal Mythology: The Psychology of Your Evolving Self*, Jeremy P. Tarcher Inc., 1988.
28. Fortune, Dion, *Aspects of Occultism*, Aquarian Press, 1962.
29. Fortune, Dion, *Moon Magic*, Aquarian Press, 1989.
30. Fortune, Dion, *The Sea Priestess*, Aquarian Press, 1989.
31. Gerald of Wales, *The History and Topography of Ireland* trans. John J. O'Meara, Penguin, 1982.
32. Gilchrist, Cherry, *The Circle of Nine*, Dryad Press, 1988.
33. Gleason, Judith, *Oya: In Praise of the Goddess*, Shambhala, 1987.
34. Graves, Robert, *Greek Myths*, Cassell, 1958.
35. Greeley, Andrew, *The Mary Myth: on the Femininity of God*, Seabury Press, 1977.
36. Gross, Rita M. 'Hindu Female Deities as a Resource for the Contemporary Rediscovery of the Goddess' in *The Book of the Goddess*, ed. Carl Olson, Crossroad, 1987.
37. Harris, Geraldine, *Gods and Pharoahs from Egyptian Mythology*, Peter Loewe, 1982.
38. Harrison, Jane, *Prolegomena to the Study of Greek Religion*, Merlin Press, 1961.
39. Hart, George, *A Dictionary of Egyptian Gods & Goddesses*, Routlege & Kegan Paul, 1986.
40. Hesiod, *The Homeric Hymns*, trans. H. G. Evelyn–White, Heinemann, 1964.
41. Hooke, S. H. *Babylonian and Assyrian Religion*, Hutchinson, 1953.
42. Howell, Alice O. *The Dove in the Stone*, Quest Books, 1988.
43. Ions, Veronica, *Egyptian Mythology*, Hamlyn, 1982.
44. Jamal, Michele, *Shape Shifters: Shaman Women in Contemporary Society*, Arkana, 1987.
45. James, M. R. *The Apocryphal New Testament*, Clarendon Press, 1924.
46. Johnson, Buffie, *Lady of the Beasts: Ancient Images of the Goddess and her Sacred Animals*, Harper & Row, 1988.
47. Jones, Prudence & Matthews, Caitlín, *Voices From the Circle: The Heritage of Western Paganism*, Aquarian Press, 1990.
48. Kerenyi, C. *The Gods of the Greeks*, Thames & Hudson, 1951.
49. Kinsley, David, *Hindu Goddesses*, University of California Press, 1988.
50. Layton, Bentley trans. *The Gnostic Scriptures*, SCM Press Ltd. 1987.
51. LeMesurier, Peter, *The Healing of the Gods*, Element Books, 1988.
52. Lindsay, Jack, *The Origins of Alchemy in Graeaco–Roman Egypt*, Frederick Muller, 1970.
53. Lovelock, James, *The Ages of Gaia: a Biography of Our Living Earth*, Oxford University Press, 1988.

54. Luke, Helen, M. *Woman; Earth and Spirit, Crossroad, 1981.*
55. Lurker, Manfred, *The Gods & Symbols of Ancient Egypt*, Thames & Hudson, 1980.
56. *The Mabinogion* trans. Lady Charlotte Guest, Ballantyne Press, 1910.
57. Marrior, Alice & Rachlin, Carol K. *American Indian Mythology*, New American Library, 1968.
58. Matthews, Caitlín, *Arthur and the Sovereignty of Britain: King and Goddess in the Mabinogion*, Arkana, 1989.
59. Matthews, Caitlín, *The Elements of the Celtic Tradition*, Element Books, 1989.
60. Matthews, Caitlín, 'In a Circle of Stone' in *Voices From the Circle*, ed. Prudence Jones & Caitlín Matthews, Aquarian Press 1990.
61. Matthews, Caitlín, *Mabon and the Mysteries of Britain: An Exploration of the Mabinogion*, Arkana, 1987.
62. Matthews, Caitlín, *The Search for Rhiannon*, Hunting Raven Press, 1981.
63. Matthews, Caitlín, *Sophia, Goddess of Wisdom: From Black Goddess to World Soul*, Unwin & Hyman, 1991.
64. Matthews, Caitlín, ed. *Voices of the Goddess: A Chorus of Sibyls*, Aquarian Press, 1990.
65. Matthews, Caitlín & John, *The Arthurian Tarot: A Hallowquest*, Aquarian Press, 1990.
66. Matthews, Caitlín & John, *The Western Way* (2 vols) Arkana, 1985, 1986.
67. Matthews, John, *Gawain, Knight of the Goddess*, Aquarian Press, 1990.
68. Meyer, Marian W. ed. *The Ancient Mysteries: a Sourcebook, Harper & Row, 1987.*
69. Monaghan, Patricia, *Women in Myth & Legend*, Junction Books, 1981.
70. Mookerjee, Ajit, *Kali: the Feminine Force*, Thames & Hudson, 1988.
71. Moore, John, *Sexuality: Spirituality*, Element Books, 1980.
72. *New Larousse Encyclopedia of Mythology*, Paul Hamlyn, 1968.
73. *Nag Hammadi Library, The*, trans. Members of the Coptic Gnostic Library Project of the Inst. for Antiquity & Christianity, dir. J. M. Robinson, Leiden, E. J. Brill, 1977.
74. Ngakpa Chögyam, *Rainbow of Liberated Energy*, Element Books, 1986.
75. O'Brien, Thesea King ed. *The Spiral Path*, Yes, 1988.
76. O'Flaherty, Wendy trans. *Hindu Myths*, Penguin, 1971.
77. O'Flaherty, Wendy, *Women, Androgynes and Other Mythical Beasts*, University of Chicago Press, 1980.
78. Olson, Carl, *The Book of the Goddess*, Crossroad, 1987.
79. Ovid, *Metamorphoses*, trans. Mary M. Innes, Penguin, 1955.
80. Patai, Raphael, *The Hebrew Goddess*, Avon Books, 1978.
81. Phillips, J. A. *Eve: The History of an Idea*, Harper & Row, 1983.
82. Plato, *The Republic* trans, Desmond Lee, Penguin, 1955.
83. Plutarch, *Moralia Vol. 5* trans. F. C. Babbitt, Heinemann, 1957.
84. Pollack, Rachel & Matthews, Caitlín, *Tarot Tales*, Century, 1989.

85. Preston, James J. ed. *Mother Worship*, Chapel Hill, University of North Carolina Press, 1982.

86. *Rig Veda* trans. Wendy D. O'Flaherty, Penguin, 1981.

87. Sharp, Cecil & Karples, Maud, ed. *The Crystal Spring*, Oxford University Press, 1975.

88. Sherab Gyaltsen Amipa, Lama, *The Opening of the Lotus: Developing Clarity and Kindness*, Wisdom Publications, 1987.

89. Seibert, Ilse, *Women in Ancient Near East*, Editions Leipzig, 1974.

90. Sjöö, Monica & Mor, Barbara, *The Great Cosmic Mother*, Harper & Row, 1987.

91. Steinbrecher, Edwin C. *The Inner Guide Meditation*, Blue Feather Press, 1978.

92. Stone, Merlin, *Ancient Mirrors of Womanhood* (2 vols) New Sibylline Books, 1979.

93. Tacitus, *The Agricola and the Germania*, trans. H. Mattingley, Penguin, 1970.

94. Thinley Norbu, *Magic Dance: the Display of the Self-Nature of the Five Wisdom Dakinis*, Jewel Publishing House, 1981.

95. *Upanishads, The*, trans. Juan Mascaró, Penguin, 1965.

96. Wilson, Martin, *In Praise of Tara: Songs to the Saviouress*, Wisdom Books, 1986.

97. Witt, R. E. *Isis in the Graeco–Roman World*, Thames & Hudson, 1971.

98. Wolkstein, Diana & Kramer, Samuel Noah, *Innana: Queen of Heaven and Earth*, Rider, 1984.

99. Wombwell, Felicity, 'The Weaving Goddess' in *Voices From the Circle* ed. Prudence Jones & Caitlín Matthews, Aquarian Press 1990.

100. Wood, Marion, *Spirits, Heroes and Hunters from North American Mythology*, Peter Loewe, 1981.

101. Zolla, Elémire, *The Androgyne: Fusion of the Sexes*, Thames & Hudson, 1981.

GODDESS LITURGY

Paxson, Diana, *The Liturgy of the Lady: the Fellowship of the Spiral Path*, MZB Enterprises, P.O. Box 72, Berkeley, CA 94701, USA.

Robertson, Olivia, *Dea: Rites and Mysteries of the Goddess: Liturgy of the Fellowship of Isis*, Cesara Publications.

Robertson, Olivia, *Pantheia: Initiations and Festivals of the Goddess*, Cesara Publications, 1988.

Robertson, Olivia, *Sophia: Cosmic Consciousness of the Goddess*, Cesara Publications.

Robertson, Olivia, *Urania: Ceremonial Magic of the Goddess*, Cesara Publications.

Winter, Miriam Therese, *Woman Prayer: Woman Song: Resources for Ritual*, Meyer Stone, 1987 (Christian feminist rituals)

USEFUL ADDRESSES

When writing to the following addresses, do not forget to enclose a stamped addressed envelope for your reply, or sufficient international reply paid coupons if you are writing from outside England or to Eire.

THE FELLOWSHIP OF ISIS, Clonegal Castle, Enniscorthy, Eire.
The Fellowship welcomes all – men and women – who love and venerate the Goddess in her many forms. Branches, temples and shrines worldwide. It publishes a quarterly newsletter and produces many other publications from the Cesara Press, see above under Olivia Robertson and Lawrence Durdin–Robertson.

THE NINE LADIES ASSOCIATION, 115d Pepys Road, London SE14. This association of women studies many aspects of myth and its practical application in daily life. It runs occasional courses and study groups.

MYSTERY WORKSHOPS, with Felicity Wombwell. Day courses about the Goddess, using the sacred creative arts of music, drama, dance and image. For finding your sacred self and exploring the cycle of the feminine within. For more details and latest leaflet, please write to Felicity Wombwell, 1 Ravenstone Road, London N8 OJT.

THE HOUSE OF NET, a priestess training programme which combines a correspondence course with periodic workshops and weekend courses. For more details write to BCM, Box 6812, London WC1N 3XX. Please enclose two first class stamps.

ARACHNE MAGAZINE, 14 Hill Crest, Sevenoaks, Kent. A magazine of Matriarchal and Goddess Studies.

MATRIARCHY NEWSLETTER, 14 Hill Crest, Sevenoaks, Kent. A feminist newsletter about the Goddess and Goddess groups in Britain. Produced at the eight festivals.

DOMUS SOPHIAE TERRAE ET SANCTE GRADALAE, BCM Hallowquest, London WCIN 3XX. For more information about training courses led by Caitlín and John Matthews in the British Mysteries, Celtic and Goddess traditions, write for details enclosing four first class stamps or two international reply paid coupons.

INDEX